Disclaimer

The information included in this book is designed to provide helpful information on the subjects discussed. This book is not meant to be used to diagnose or treat any medical condition. For diagnosis or treatment of any medical problem, consult your own doctor. The author and publisher are not responsible for any specific health or allergy needs that may require medical supervision and are not liable for any damages or negative consequences from any application, action, treatment, or preparation, to anyone reading or following the information in this book. Links may change and any references included are provided for informational purposes only.

Crock-Pot Recipes

125 World-Class Slow Cooker Recipes

By Susan Hollister
Copyright © 2017

Table of Contents

CHAPTER 6: CROCK-POT PASTA, RICE AND GRAIN RECIPES TO DIE FOR 75

CHAPTER 7: DELICIOUS VEGETARIAN DISHES THAT EVERYONE LOVES..89

CHAPTER 10: SWEET AND SPICY SAUCES AND CONDIMENTS.. 127

CONCLUSION 140

MY OTHER BOOKS... 141

Introduction

I don't know how any family survives without a Crock-Pot or slow cooker. They save time, cut costs and are so easy to use anyone can make a meal fit for a king in one. Today, most moms and dads both work and once they pick up the kids and get home, they are exhausted. Most of the time, they pick up burgers or pizza on the way home rather than spend the time to cook a meal. If you get off work at 5 pm and it takes until 6 to get home, the family would not even start to eat until 7:30 or 8:00 pm. When you use a Crock-Pot, you can make dinner the night before in the pot and refrigerate overnight. The next morning pop it in the Crock-Pot shell, turn it to low and let it cook all day while you are at work. When you get home at 6, dinner is almost ready. It only takes a few minutes to get it on the table. Slow Cookers make it easy to serve a home cooked dinner that is healthy and delicious.

Cook just about anything in a Crock-Pot from appetizers, side dishes, main dishes, seafood, desserts and even condiments and sauces. It is hard to burn anything in a Crock-Pot and if you use nonstick spray or liners, there is little clean up required. Use it for dinner, for potlucks, for parties, at barbeques and anywhere else food is served. You can serve the dish right out of the Crock-Pot instead of involving other dishes.

Food in a Crock-Pot cooks slowly and meats are more likely to be tender and delicious because of the low heat and long cooking time. The ingredients get to meld together better and longer for more flavor and better taste. Nothing dries out so meats are juicy and delectable.

This book has 125 recipes from which to choose. There are over 61 main dish recipes in this book and most of the 12 soups and stews can also be used as main dishes as well. The 12 breakfast and lunch recipes are easily adapted to dinner dishes. You have 13 appetizers to choose from and 14 desserts and other sweet treats. Probably my favorite recipes in the book include:

- Cranberry sauce, which is so much easier to make in a Crock-Pot than on the stove and it won't burn.
- Salisbury Steak because it tastes better than the entre at a restaurant
- The Buffalo Chicken Dip because you can make a sandwich out of it, but it is just better to eat it right out of the crock with a spoon.
- The meaty spaghetti sauce because everyone loves it.
- The pineapple upside down cake, just because it tastes delicious.

It is really hard to pick a favorite because all the recipes produce A+ dishes that will impress your friends and family.

It doesn't matter what you call them. Crock-Pots and slow cookers are exactly the same thing; it just depends on the brand. The inside part is the crock and made from stoneware. Remember the old fashioned crocks grandma used to make corned beef or pickles. The crocks in the are made from a similar material. This is the part that is easily removed and put in the refrigerator and washed. Crock material helps either keep things cool or hot because it has insulating qualities. Pioneers put butter in crocks and it kept the butter cool. When applying heat to the crock, it stays evenly hot and things inside cook better.

The crock or stone part of the pot slides into a metal sleeve and base. The pot is electric and a heating element in the bottom causes the heat to rise up the sides of the crock. Most Crock-Pots have high and low settings and some have a warm setting. Depending on the model, they may even have a timer. Most dishes need to be cooked at least 8 hours on low and 4 hours on high. The timer comes in handy if you aren't going to be home in 8 hours. Just set the timer to turn off after the desired amount of time.

The lid of the Crock-Pot is very important. It is made of glass and must be on for the Crock-Pot to work properly. The lid does not allow liquid to escape from the pot and evaporate, so the food inside stays moist. You almost always use the Crock-Pot with the lid on, but sometimes the ingredients in the Crock-Pot need to thicken. In this case, you would cook with the lid off. This allows the steam and liquid to evaporate and the food inside thickens.

Crock-Pots come in many different sizes. My favorites are the large oblong types that come in 4, 5 or 7-quart. The 7-quart is essential for a family. I like the oblongs because a chicken, roast or ham will fit in easily. The round types might not allow these things to fit very well. The round ones are normally in the 4 to 5-quart size, and they make even smaller ones for 1 person.

Using the right size Crock-Pot is essential to having a cooked meal when you want it. If you put a large recipe in a small Crock-Pot, it takes longer to cook. You might find the meat isn't done and that can cause food poisoning. Most recipes are formulated for a 5 to 6-quart Crock-Pot. If you have a larger one, you may find you don't have to cook it for as long as the recipe says. Crock-Pots should only be filled 2/3 of the capacity in the crock so that food cooks evenly. Overstuffing a Crock-Pot can lead to disaster.

I highly recommend Crock-Pots that have a probe and thermometer. You just insert the probe and you can see the temperature of the food to make sure it is right. If your Crock-Pot does not have a probe, I recommend a digital food thermometer. When the food is ready, just pop off the lid and take the temperature. If it isn't done, replace the lid and cook a little longer. I have seen a floatable, stainless steel thermometer that can either be inserted or floated in the Crock-Pot and you can sort of see it through the clear lid unless condensation has gathered. In most cases, food will cook in the time allotted on the recipe, but if you want to be safe, test it first.

Some people think the only thing you can cook in a Crock-Pot or slow cooker is main dishes. Not so!!!! Cook just about anything in them from stews and soups to vegetable dishes, eggs and sausage, pasta and even dessert. A Crock-Pot makes a very good gift for the college student living in a dorm. Get that and a small refrigerator and they will be set.

The only problem I had when I first started to convert my regular recipes to slow cooker recipes is that I forgot liquid does not evaporate like it does in a regular pan on the stove or in a casserole in the oven. You use LESS liquid because it does not evaporate. That is the only rule you must remember when using the Crock-Pot. An example would be a recipe that asked for 4 cups of chicken stock. Instead of 4 cups, cut it to 2 cups and see how it does. The only time that doesn't work is when the other stuff in the Crock-Pot absorbs liquid like beans, rice and pasta. Then you use the regular amount. Another suggestion is to use Crock-Pot liners if you are making something that is going to be sticky. These liners come in all different sizes and save you time because you don't have to soak or scrape the crock out when you are done using it. Just give it a rinse and you are ready for the next time you want to use it.

I like to prepare my meal the night before I put it on in the morning. I do not like getting up early to chop meat and vegetables. You can put the ingredients in the Crock-Pot and put the crock part and lid in the refrigerator overnight, but this makes the crock cold. Therefore, it takes longer for the crock to heat up and you must add an extra hour to the cooking time. Here is a way to prepare for the day to come without adding additional cooking time.

Chop your meat and brown it, if necessary. Let it cook and put it into a dish and cover with foil or plastic wrap. Prepare chopped vegetables and herbs and place them in re-closeable plastic bags or dishes covered with plastic wrap. In the morning, put your liner in or spray the crock and start dumping everything in the crock as you would normally. You might have a few extra dishes, but it is worth it.

I don't know how many times I have transported my Crock-Pot to church or to a friend's house and had a problem with leakage. The lid of the Crock-Pot is not secure and when in a car, it can slide off. You can get a Crock-Pot lid lock that fits over the lid and keeps it solidly in place. It won't leak at all. Some lid locks have a ladle that slides in too making it very convenient for serving.

Travel bags are also handy. Your Crock-Pot is usually hot when you transport it and it is not easy to handle. There are insulated cloth bags that zip open. You just place the Crock-Pot, lid and all, inside and zip it up. No burning your hands on the Crock-Pot. I still secure the lid with a lid lock too. My travel bag has a shoulder handle so I can sling it over my shoulder to carry it.

An essential accessory is the rack. I have seen round Crock-Pots that do have a rack for the bottom of the Crock-Pot, but more likely, the oval ones will have them. The racks look somewhat like a cooling rack. The fit in the bottom and raise food about ½ inch to an inch above the bottom. This comes in handy when cooking something with greasy meat so it keeps the grease away from the food you are going to eat. I have a rack for my oval Crock-Pot that has long handles on the side. They come up almost to the lid so I can lift out whatever is in there without putting my hands in to get burned. I love that rack.

Enjoy letting the Crock-Pot or slow cooker do all the work for you with the recipes in this book. You will enjoy a variety of incredible recipes from appetizers to desserts along with delicious breakfast, lunch and dinner recipes that will please your family and visitors. Enjoy.

Chapter 1: Crock-Pot Appetizers That Will Be the Life of the Party

Appetizers are a great way to get a party going, but they don't need a party to be enjoyed. Fix a few appetizers for the family and serve them before dinner or have an all appetizer feast instead of dinner one day. Appetizers can be anything small from dips to tiny meatballs and wings. They are a great way to get the appetite going and hold everyone over until dinner is served. Many of the following recipes can be served right out of the Crock-Pot or slow cooker. Serve them at your next dinner party, Super Bowl party or before dinner.

BBQ Crock-Pot Kielbasa
Polish sausage is another word for kielbasa and it is a pork sausage that is a little spicy. When you combine it with the sauce in the recipe, it almost comes out like a sweet candy coating and it is so good it is hard to stop eating. Make sure to spray the Crock-Pot well with nonstick spray or the sauce will set up like concrete.

Ingredients:
1/4 cup horseradish
1/2 cup ketchup
1 cup packed brown sugar
2 pounds kielbasa

Directions:
1. Prepare the Crock-Pot with nonstick spray.

2. In a bowl, whisk the horseradish and ketchup together and add the brown sugar mixing well.

3. Slice the kielbasa in thin rounds and layer them on the bottom of the Crock-Pot. Pour the sauce over top and stir just a little to coat all the rounds.

4. Cook on high until the mixture starts to boil on the sides, about 1 to 1-1/2 hour.

5. Reduce to low and cook about 1 hour or until the sauce thickens.

Buffalo Chicken Dip in a Slow Cooker

Serve hot or cold and with pita chips, tortilla chips, crackers, little rounds of bread and anything else you can think of. I have a hard time not taking a spoon to the slow cooker and eating it right out of there.

Ingredients:
16 ounces cream cheese, softened and cut into cubes
1/4 cup hot sauce
1 cup prepared ranch dressing
2 cups cooked shredded chicken (about 1 whole breast)
2 cups shredded sharp Cheddar cheese

Directions:
1. Spray the slow cooker with nonstick spray.

2. In a medium bowl, mix the cream cheese, hot sauce and ranch dressing and pour into the slow cooker.

3. Cook on low for 2 hours stirring every ½ hour.

4. Add the chicken and cheese and cook 1 more hour stirring at least twice so the cheese does not burn.

5. Serve right in the slow cooker with the dial set to warm

Crock-Pot Ham Meatballs

Those that enjoy cranberry glaze on a ham will absolutely love these ham meatballs. They are a little different that beef meatballs and will definitely cause a frenzy at the appetizer table.

Ingredients:
1 beaten egg
2 tablespoons dried cranberries
1/2 cup pulverized graham crackers
1/4 teaspoon ground cloves
1/4 cup peeled and finely chopped onion
2 tablespoons milk
12 ounces ground pork
12 ounces ground fully cooked ham, ground

1 teaspoon olive oil
1 tablespoon vinegar
1 (16-oz) can jellied cranberry sauce
1 (12-oz) bottle chili sauce
1/2 teaspoon dry mustard

Directions:
1. In a bowl, beat the egg well. Cut the cranberries up with scissors and add to the beaten egg along with the graham cracker crumbs, cloves, onion, milk, pork and ham.

2. Use hands to mix well together and form into small meatballs. It will make about 75.

3. In a skillet brown the meatballs in olive oil over medium heat. Cook almost all the way through and remove draining on paper towels.

4. In a sauce pan combine the vinegar, cranberry sauce, chili sauce and mustard heating over medium. Cook until cranberry sauce melts and the mixture becomes smooth.

5. Prepare a Crock-Pot with nonstick spray and place the drained meatballs in the bottom. Pour the sauce over top.

6. Cover and cook on high for 3 hours. Reduce to warm and serve from the Crock-Pot.

Crock-Pot Hot Crab Dip
Use a can of flaked crab with this dish. Serve with crackers or pita chips for a delightful seafood dip.

Ingredients:
3/4 cup Parmesan Cheese, shredded
1-1/2 tablespoons Worcestershire Sauce
2 – 8 ounce packages of cream cheese, softened
3/4 cup mayonnaise
1/4 cup green onions that have been sliced very thin
2 – 6 ounce cans of crab flaked crab meat, cartilage removed, drained well
Fresh chives, chopped

Directions:

1. Spray the Crock-Pot with nonstick spray.

2. Mix the Parmesan, Worcestershire sauce, cream cheese, and mayonnaise in a bowl. Add the green onions and mix in well.

3. Use a fork to work the mixture together very well.

4. Pour the mixture into the Crock-Pot and cook on low 2 hours. Sprinkled top with chopped chives and switch to warm to serve.

Crock-Pot Mexican Hamburger Dip
Anyone who likes tacos will love this dip. It is a little spicy because of the jalapeno, chili powder, chili peppers and chili sauce. If you don't want something spicy, replace the jalapeno with a green bell pepper, omit the chili peppers, cut down on the chili powder and add ketchup instead of chili sauce.

Ingredients:

2 pounds ground beef
1 jalapeno pepper, seeded and minced
1 small onion, chopped
2 cloves garlic, crushed
1-4 ounce can mild chili peppers
1-1/2 teaspoon chili powder
½ teaspoon pepper
¼ teaspoon salt
½ teaspoon ground cumin
½ cup chili sauce
2-8 ounce cans tomato sauce
1 teaspoon sugar
1 teaspoon oregano
16 ounces cream cheese, cut in cubes and softened
½ cup shredded Monterey Jack cheese

Directions:

1. In a skillet, over medium heat, brown the ground beef with the jalapeno, onion and garlic added. Once browned, drain and put this mixture into the Crock-Pot.

2. Add the chili peppers, chili powder, pepper, salt, cumin, chili sauce, tomato sauce, sugar and oregano and mix.

3. Add the cream cheese cubes and Monterey Jack cheese over top and cook on low for 2 hours.

4. Serve right out of the Crock-Pot with crackers or tortilla chips.

Crock-Pot Nachos

This recipe is even good for dinner or provide a snack during movie night at home.

Ingredients:
1 tablespoon chili powder
1 tablespoon cumin
1 tablespoon garlic powder
1 teaspoon salt
1 teaspoon pepper
1 small onion, peeled and chopped
1 – can Chipotle peppers, chopped
1 – (4-oz) can green chilies, drained and diced
5 cups chicken broth
4 pounds boneless and skinless chicken thighs
1 tablespoon granulated sugar
1 tablespoon water
Tortilla chips
Shredded cheddar cheese
Lettuce
Olives
Diced tomatoes
Sour cream

Directions:
1. In a small bowl combine the dried spices including salt and pepper and set it aside.

2. Prepare a Crock-Pot with nonstick spray and place the onion, Chipotle peppers and green chilies in the bottom.

3. Pour the broth over top.

4. Rub the chicken with the spice mixture reserving about 1 tablespoon. Place the chicken in the Crock-Pot.

5. Cook on high for 6 hours or low for 8 hours and remove the chicken shredding with two forks.

6. Pour tortilla chips on a large platter and layer on 2 cups of the shredded chicken, shredded Cheddar, tomatoes, olives etc.

7. In a small bowl, combine the rest of the dry seasoning mix with the sugar and water. Mix well and drizzle over the Nachos.

8. Serve with sour cream.

Easy Reuben Dip
Anyone who likes Reuben sandwiches with corned beef and sauerkraut will love this dip. Use deli corned beef cut into small pieces and serve this dip right from the Crock-Pot on crackers or rye rounds.

Ingredients:
16-ounce brick of cream cheese, softened
16-ounce carton of sour cream
1 (27-oz) can sauerkraut, drained
½ pound deli sliced corned beef
2 (8-oz) packages shredded Swiss cheese

Directions:
1. In a mixer bowl, beat the softened cream cheese and the sour cream until creamy.

2. Add the drained sauerkraut and beat in.

3. Chop the deli sliced corned beef in small pieces and add with the Swiss cheese. Mix by hand.

4. Prepare a Crock-Pot with nonstick spray.

5. Pour the dip in and let it cook on low 2 to 3 hours or until it all gets melted and gooey.

Pepper Dip With Pale Ale

Those that like the flavor of pale ale will love this recipe. Serve this dip with tortilla chips and I promise it will be a hit.

Ingredients:
1/2 teaspoon onion powder
1/2 teaspoon ground cumin
1/2 teaspoon chili powder
1/4 teaspoon pepper
1/4 teaspoon salt
12 ounces cream cheese, softened
3/4 cup sour cream
2 cloves garlic, peeled and minced
1 jalapeño pepper, seeded, stemmed and minced
1 red bell pepper, seeded, stemmed and diced
3-1/2 cups frozen corn
1-1/2 cup shredded Monterey Jack cheese
1/2 cup pale ale beer
5 strips bacon
Green onions

Directions:
1. In a small bowl, combine the onion powder, cumin, chili powder, pepper and salt. Set aside.

2. In another bowl mix the cream cheese and sour cream and add the herbs and spices already mixed in the small bowl. Mix in with a fork.

3. Spray the Crock-Pot with nonstick spray and layer both peppers, corn and Monterey Jack cheese inside.

4. Add the cream cheese and herb mixture to the Crock-Pot and pour the ale over top.

5. Cook for 6 to 8 hours on low or 4 to 5 hours on high.

6. While cooking, fry the bacon, drain on paper towels and let it cool, then break into small pieces.

7. Chop the chives for garnish.

8. Stir everything together before serving and sprinkle on the bacon and chives.

Pepperoni Dip Slow Cooker Style

Serve on whole wheat crackers or little rounds of bread. There are only 3 ingredients, so how hard can this be.

Ingredients:
7 ounces of sliced pepperoni
8 ounces softened cream cheese
1 (10.5-oz) cream of celery soup

Directions:
1. Prepare the slow cooker with non-stick spray.

2. Cut all the slices of pepperoni in half and put them in the slow cooker.

3. Slice cream cheese into chunks and put on top of the pepperoni.

4. Scrape the soup out of the can and spread evenly on top.

5. Cook on low about 1 hour, stirring every once in a while. Keep on warm to serve.

Slow Cooker Hot Onion Dip

My family has always been a fan of onion dip served cold with wavy potato chips, but this hot version is even better. Serve with chips, bread rounds, pita chips or pretzels. Add some cooked and broken bacon, ham, green onions or anything else that sounds good the last 15 minutes of cooking

Ingredients:
1 teaspoon olive oil
1 medium onion, peeled and finely chopped
1-1/2 cups shredded or grated Parmesan
16 ounces cubed and softened cream cheese

Directions:

1. Add the olive oil to a skillet heated on medium high heat.

2. Sauté the onion for about 3 to 4 minutes.

3. Prepare the slow cooker with nonstick spray and place the onion on the bottom.

4. Sprinkle the Parmesan over the onion and then add the cubed cream cheese on top of all.

5. Cook 2 hours stirring every half hour and serve keeping the dip warm.

Slow Cooker Marinated Mushrooms

Marinated mushrooms are a favorite at my house and these are really good and very easy to make in your slow cooker. You do start out making this recipe on the stove but you will only dirty 1 pan and a knife.

Ingredients:
1 cup dry red wine
1 cup chicken broth
1 cup beef broth
1 teaspoon dill
1 teaspoon garlic powder
1 teaspoon Worcestershire sauce
4 pounds fresh mushrooms
1/2 cup butter

Directions:
1. Bring to boil in a saucepan the red wine, chicken and beef broths.

2. Add the dill, garlic powder and Worcestershire sauce and stir to combine.

3. Remove the stems from the mushrooms and chop.

4. Layer the mushrooms on the bottom of the crock and add the stems over top.

5. Pour the broth/wine mixture over top and top off with the butter.

6. Cook on low for about 8 hours and serve.

Slow Cooked Spicy Chicken Wings
If you like a sweet and sour flavor for wings, you will love this appetizer done in the slow cooker. Serve it at football games and make sure to have plenty of napkins on hand.

Ingredients:
5 to 6 pounds chicken wings, split and tips removed
1/4 cup molasses
1 tablespoon commercial salsa
1 (12-oz) bottle chili sauce
1-1/2 tablespoon Worcestershire sauce
1/4 cup fresh squeezed lemon juice
3 drops hot sauce
1 teaspoon garlic powder
1/4 teaspoon salt
2 teaspoons chili powder

Directions:
1. Place the wings in a nonstick sprayed slow cooker.

2. In a bowl, combine the molasses, salsa, chili sauce, Worcestershire sauce, lemon juice, hot sauce, garlic powder, salt and chili powder and whisk with a wire whisk.

3. Pour over the wings and cook on low for 5 hours and serve.

Zingy Jalapeno and Corn Dip
This is one spicy dip and your guests will be asking for more and more. It has the smoky flavor of bacon with Pepper Jack cheese and sour cream and that kick of jalapeno. Serve it with plain crackers so you can enjoy all the dip flavors.

Ingredients:
4 slices of bacon
3 (15-oz) cans whole kernel corn, drained
2 jalapeno peppers, seeded and diced fine
1 cup shredded Pepper Jack cheese

½ cup sour cream
¼ cup grated Parmesan cheese
Salt and pepper to taste
1 (8-oz) brick cream cheese, cut in cubes
2 tablespoons fresh chives or cilantro

Directions:

1. In a skillet prepared with nonstick spray, fry the bacon until brown. Drain on paper towel and set aside.

2. Place in the Crock-Pot, the corn, jalapenos, Pepper Jack cheese, sour cream, Parmesan cheese and salt and pepper. Stir and top with the cubes of cream cheese.

3. Cook on low for 2 hours.

4. Dice the bacon and throw it in the Crock-Pot. Stir and cook on high 15 minutes.

5. Sprinkle with chives or cilantro right before serving and leave the Crock-Pot on warm.

Chapter 2: Slow Cooker Soups and Stews That Warm the Body and Soul

Autumn is when we break out the slow cooker and make soup or stew at least once a week. Soups warm the body when you aren't quite used to that cold weather coming on and once it does, soup makes one of the best wintertime meals around. Make soups and stews from beef, lamb, chicken and vegetables. They are healthy and easy to make in a slow cooker.

Chicken Noodle Soup in a Crock-Pot
I love making chicken soup in a Crock-Pot because it is so much easier than making it in a stock pot on the stove. You don't have to worry about anything sticking and burning to the bottom of the pot, because nothing is worse than burned soup. This soup is good for whatever ails you. Even if you have a cold, it takes little effort to make a soup that will help you feel better.

Ingredients:
1 small onion, peeled and chopped
3 stalks celery, chopped
2 carrots, peeled and chopped
3 pounds chicken pieces
4 cups chicken broth
4 cups water
Salt and pepper to taste
1 tablespoon garlic, minced
1/2 teaspoon dried marjoram
1/4 cup fresh chopped parsley
1 bay leaf
6 ounces medium egg noodles

Directions:
1. Peel and chop the onion, celery and carrots and place in the bottom of a Crock-Pot prepared by spraying with nonstick spray.

2. Place the uncooked chicken pieces on top and pour in the broth and water.

3. Add salt and pepper, garlic, marjoram, parsley and bay leaf.

4. Cook 5 to 6 hours on low.

5. Remove the bay leaf and the chicken. Remove the chicken from the bone and dice placing it back in the Crock-Pot when done.

6. Add dry noodles and cook for 45 more minutes on low, or turn to high and cook about 20 more minutes. Once the noodles are tender, the soup is ready to serve.

Chicken Sweet Potato Stew

This stew is sweet and spicy with the chorizo and allspice. It is a flavorful stew that has a distinctive taste and most people like it. I'm not sure, but I think the origin is in Africa because I got the recipe from a woman that came from Algeria and the people in parts of Africa do cook with sweet potatoes, although they are a little different than the ones we have here. What confuses me is the chorizo, which is a Spanish-type food. Maybe it was just added to give the stew some more flavor.

Ingredients:
2 medium sweet potatoes
2 boneless chicken breasts
1 pound chorizo
2 cloves garlic, minced
1 large onion, peeled and chopped
1 (15-oz) can garbanzo beans, drained
1 (28-oz) can whole tomatoes, with the juice
1 teaspoon paprika
½ teaspoon allspice
½ teaspoon cumin
1 teaspoon salt
1 teaspoon pepper
2 tablespoons tomato paste
Fresh parsley for garnish, chopped

Directions:
1. Prepare Crock-Pot with nonstick spray.

2. Peel sweet potatoes and dice in 1 inch cubes.

3. Cut chicken and chorizo in 1 inch pieces.

4. Layer in the crock, the potatoes, chicken, chorizo, garlic, onion, beans, tomatoes with juice, paprika, allspice, cumin, salt pepper and top with tomato paste.

5. Cook on low for 5 hours and serve.

Crock-Pot Broccoli and Three Cheese Soup

I usually do not like processed cheese, but in this soup, it would taste right without it. I use Velveeta because I think it tastes better than most cheeses of this type. Two other cheeses are used in this soup with broccoli and they are Cheddar and Parmesan, but you can try shredded Swiss or Fontanel cheese if you like.

Ingredients:
1/4 cup butter
1 tablespoon garlic, minced
1 large yellow onion, peeled and chopped
1/4 cup flour
1 (12-oz) can evaporated milk
4 cups chicken broth
1/2 teaspoon salt
1/2 teaspoon pepper
1 (14-oz) bag of frozen baby broccoli florets, thawed and drained
1 (8-oz) loaf of processed cheese product (Velveeta)
1 -1/2 cups shredded Cheddar
1 cup shredded Parmesan cheese

Directions:
1. In a skillet over medium high heat, melt the butter.

2. Sauté the garlic and onion for 4 minutes.

3. Sprinkle the flour over the garlic and onion and stir constantly for about 1 minute then add the evaporated milk in a slow stream and whisk with a wire whisk until the liquid is smooth.

4. Pour into a Crock-Pot that is treated with nonstick spray.

5. Add the broth, salt, pepper and frozen broccoli. Cook on low for 4 hours or until it starts to bubble.

6. Slice the processed cheese loaf into cubes and put them in the Crock-Pot with the other two cheeses. Stir until everything melts. The soup is ready to serve.

Crock-Pot Cream of Potato Soup

Potato soup is comfort food. My mom used to make it on cold winter nights because it stuck to your ribs. What I did not know at the time is that it is also cheap to make and that is why we had it at the end of a pay period. Mom always had to watch the pot carefully so that the soup didn't burn on the bottom. I do not have to do that because I use my Crock-Pot. Variations abound with potato soup. Instead of bacon, use some leftover ham chunks. If you like cheese, add 1 or 2 cups of shredded cheddar before serving and let it melt for a few minutes. Garnish your soup with chives. I have some growing in my kitchen window and they give it some extra punch.

Ingredients:
1 teaspoon olive oil
1 sweet onion, peeled and finely chopped
2 teaspoons garlic, minced
6 slices of bacon
2 cups water
2 (10.5-oz) cans of chicken broth
1/2 teaspoon salt
1/2 teaspoon cracked pepper
5 to 6 potatoes, peeled and diced
1/2 cup flour
2 cups half and half
1 (12 fluid-oz) can of evaporated milk
1 tablespoon dried parsley

Directions:
1. Heat a skillet over medium high heat and add the olive oil. Add the onion and garlic and sauté for about 4 minutes.

2. Add bacon that has been cut into ½ inch pieces and cook until it is brown and crisp. Remove the bacon, onion and garlic to drain on a paper towel.

3. Once drained, place the bacon mixture in the bottom of a Crock-Pot treated with nonstick spray.

4. Stir in the water and the broth and then add the salt and pepper.

5. Pour in the diced potatoes and cook on low for at least 7 hours and no more than 8.

6. About ½ hour before serving, mix the flour and half and half in a bowl by whisking it well. Stir this into the Crock-Pot with the potatoes and then add the evaporated milk and parsley. Let this cook on high for the last ½ hour.

7. The soup should thicken.

Crock-Pot Irish Lamb Stew
Leeks look like big green onions. They must be washed thoroughly because mud and dirt gets up in between the layers and stays there. You must separate the leaves and clean well and you only use the white part of the leek. The leek has a milder flavor than green onions and it has a different texture too. Anyone who likes lamb will enjoy this stew. Make sure to get a boneless leg of lamb to make things easier.

Ingredients:
3 large leeks, white part only
1-1/2 pounds potatoes peeled and cut in 1 inch pieces
3 stalks celery, thinly sliced
3 large carrots, peeled and sliced in 1 inch chunks
1 (14-oz) can chicken broth
1 teaspoon salt
1 teaspoon pepper
2 teaspoon fresh thyme, chopped
2 pounds boneless leg of lamb, trimmed and cut in 1 inch pieces
1/4 cup fresh parsley, chopped

Directions:

1. Cut off the green part of the leak and discard it. Separate leaves and wash the white part well.

2. Prepare a Crock-Pot with nonstick spray and place the leak pieces at the bottom.

3. Layer the potatoes, celery and carrots next.

4. Add the broth, salt, pepper and thyme and layer the lamb on top.

5. Cook low 8 hours.

6. Before serving, add the parsley and cook 15 more minutes on high. Serve.

Easy Crock-Pot Beef Stew
The beef is cooked for so long, you probably won't even have to chew it because it is so tender. This is my family's favorite beef stew. Once you try it, you will never go back to making it on the stove.

Ingredients:
1 tablespoon olive oil
1 clove of garlic, minced
1 medium sweet onion, peeled and diced
2 stalks celery, chopped
4 large carrots, peeled and sliced
1 more tablespoon olive oil
1/4 cup flour
1/2 teaspoon salt
1/2 teaspoon pepper
1 teaspoon paprika
2 pounds stew beef, cubed
1 bay leaf
1 teaspoon Worcestershire sauce
1-1/2 cups beef broth
3 large potatoes, peeled and diced

Directions:
1. In a skillet, heat 1 tablespoon olive oil over medium heat and sauté the garlic, onion, celery and carrots for 4

minutes. Pour into the bottom of a nonstick sprayed Crock-Pot.

2. Add the other tablespoon of olive oil to the skillet.

3. In a medium bowl combine the flour, salt, pepper and paprika. Add the beef and toss to lightly coat.

4. Pour beef into the heated skillet and brown on all sides. Place the beef into the Crock-Pot and sprinkle over any leftover flour mixture with the bay leaf in the Crock-Pot.

5. Add the Worcestershire sauce, broth and potatoes and stir.

6. Cook on low 10 to 12 hours or on high 4 to 6 hours. The stew will thicken as it cooks.

7. Remove the bay leaf before serving.

French Onion Soup Crock-Pot Style

I love the flavor of French onion soup because of the richness that develops when you cook it for a long time. This soup is perfect for the Crock-Pot. That rich flavor comes through very well. Make the soup part and at the end you float a slice of French Bread on top with Gruyere cheese melted on top. Now I'm hungry! The alcohol in the sherry may not boil out because of the slow cooking. If you would rather not use it, increase the broth to 6 cups and omit the sherry.

Ingredients:
1/4 cup unsalted butter
1 teaspoon dried thyme
1 bay leaf
5 pounds large sweet onions (16 cups)
1 tablespoon sugar
2 tablespoons red wine vinegar
5-1/2 cups beef stock
1/2 teaspoon kosher salt
1 teaspoon pepper
½ cup sherry
24 slices of French bread (use a baguette)

5 ounces or about 1 -14 cups shredded Gruyere cheese

Directions:

1. Prepare the Crock-Pot by spraying with nonstick spray and cut the butter into small pieces layering them on the bottom of the crock.

2. Place the thyme and bay leaf in the Crock-Pot.

3. Peel the onions and slice thinly vertically. They will cook down better sliced this way.

4. Add the onions on top of the butter and herbs sprinkling them with the sugar. The sugar will caramelize the onions in the Crock-Pot. No need to do it in a skillet. Cook on low for 8 hours.

5. Fish out the bay leaf and throw it away. Add the vinegar, stock, salt and pepper and cook for 30 more minutes on high.

6. During the last 30 minutes, preheat the broiler of your oven to high and cover 2 baking sheets with foil. Place the slices of French bread in a single layer and place in the broiler for 30 seconds on both sides. You need them to be slightly toasty on the outside and soft on the inside.

7. Place 1 cup of soup into each of 12 oven-proof bowls or ramekins. Place the bread on top (2 pieces if it will fit) and about 2 tablespoons of shredded Gruyere on top.

8. Place the ramekins on a jellyroll pan and broil for 2 minutes or until the cheese melts and browns. Serve right away.

Ham and Lentil Crock-Pot Soup
This is a hearty soup with the earthy flavor of lentils and smoky flavor of ham. It is very satisfying. You put the lentils in dry, no soaking overnight, and they cook in 11 hours.

Ingredients:
1 cup dried lentils
1 cup celery, diced

1 cup carrots, chopped
1 cup onion, peeled and chopped
2 cloves garlic, peeled and minced
1-1/2 cup cooked ham, diced
½ teaspoon dry basil
¼ teaspoon dry thyme
½ teaspoon dry oregano
1 bay leaf
¼ teaspoon black pepper
32 ounces chicken broth
1 cup water
8 teaspoons tomato sauce

Directions:

1. Prepare Crock-Pot by spraying with nonstick spray.

2. Layer lentils, celery, carrots, onion, garlic, ham, dry herbs and pepper in the Crock-Pot.

3. Pour over the chicken broth and water.

4. Place the tomato sauce over all.

5. Cook on low for 11 hours. Lentils should become soft by then. Find the bay leaf and discard and serve.

Homemade Beef and Barley Soup in a Slow Cooker
Make this soup in just minutes before you head out to work, or prepare the slow cooker before you go to bed, put the crock in the refrigerator overnight and pop it into the metal sleeve in the morning. When you get home, you have piping hot soup that is good served with a crusty bread.

Ingredients:
2 tablespoons olive oil
1 tablespoon garlic, peeled and minced
1 small onion, peeled and chopped
6 large carrots peeled and chopped
4 stalks of celery that have been chopped
1 tablespoon more of olive oil
1-1/2 pounds lean beef that has been cubed

1/2 teaspoon salt
1/2 teaspoon pepper
6 cups water
3 (10.5-oz) cans of beef broth
1 cup barley
1 teaspoon dried thyme

Directions:

1. In a skillet, add the olive oil over medium heat and sauté the garlic and onion.

2. Add the carrot and celery and sauté for 4 minutes. Pour into a slow cooker prepared with nonstick spray.

3. Place 1 tablespoon of olive oil in the same skillet and start browning the beef on all sides. Add the salt and pepper.

4. Once browned, place the beef in the slow cooker.

5. Add the water and half the beef broth to the slow cooker.

6. Pour the other half of the broth into the skillet and scrape to get all the brown bits up and pour all into the slow cooker.

7. Add the barley and cook on low for 6 to 8 hours.

8. Add the thyme 15 minutes before ready to serve.

Incredible Chicken Stew

Stew is a traditional meal that doesn't cost much money and stretches the food dollar. My mother used to make kitchen sink stew. She would save even the tiniest bit of leftovers from the week and on Friday or Saturday pour it all into a pot with some broth and she made stew. I will admit this wasn't the best meal, but it kept you from being hungry.

I like to serve this Crock-Pot stew over baking soda biscuits that I make earlier and either warm up in the microwave, or just throw them in the oven covered with foil for 20 minutes at 350. It is just as incredible with some crackers or crusty bread.

Ingredients:
1/3 cup water

1 (10.75-oz) can cream of mushroom soup
1 teaspoon salt
1/2 teaspoon pepper
1/2 teaspoon garlic powder
4 chicken leg quarters with skin removed, the thigh removed from the leg
2 medium onions, peeled and chopped
1 cup frozen corn, thawed and drained
3 medium potatoes, peeled and cubed
1 (8-oz) can tomato sauce
1 envelope onion soup mix

Directions:

1. Prepare the Crock-Pot by spraying with nonstick spray.

2. Measure out the water into the Crock-Pot and add the contents of the can of cream of mushroom soup.

3. Add in the salt, pepper and garlic powder and whisk until smooth.

4. Put the chicken pieces in and cook on high for 1 hour.

5. Add the chopped onions, corn, potatoes and tomato sauce to the crock.

6. Sprinkle over the envelop of onion soup and put the cover back on cooking on low 6 to 8 more hours or 4 hours on high.

7. Pull out the chicken with a slotted spoon and shred with two forks removing the bones. Put it back in, stir the stew and serve.

Slow Cooker Cider and Pork Stew

Cider stew is an autumn favorite. We look forward to Halloween because this is the dish we serve. Kids go trick or treating early in our town; around 4 pm and are done by 6 or so. The kids in our family enjoy this stew about as much as they like the candy they got.

Some people are afraid to do anything with pork shoulder, but it is seriously easy to prepare. Just trim all the fat off and cut the meat in ½ inch wide sections. You can just as easily cube the meat, but we like it shredded and shred it with 2 forks putting it back in to the Crock-Pot when we are done.

Ingredients:
3 tablespoons flour
1/4 teaspoon dried thyme
1 teaspoon salt
1 teaspoon pepper
2 pounds boneless pork shoulder
1/4 teaspoon dried thyme
1 cup peeled and chopped yellow onion
4 medium potatoes, peeled and cubed
6 carrots, peeled and cut in coins
2 cups apple cider
1 tablespoon vinegar
1/2 cup cold water
1/4 cup more of flour

Directions:
1. Combine the flour, thyme, salt and pepper in a medium bowl and whisk to mix it well. Add the pork sections or cubes and toss to coat all the meat.

2. Prepare a slow cooker by spraying the sides and bottom with nonstick spray.

3. Put the onion, carrots and potatoes in the bottom of the slow cooker and layer the floured meat on top.

4. Pour the apple cider and the vinegar in a large glass measuring cup and whisk together. Slowly pour it over the contents in the slow cooker.

5. Cook on low 9 to 11 hours. (I have tried to cook on high 4 to 5 hours, but it does not tenderize the meat as well)

6. Turn the slow cooker on high and remove the pork and shred it with 2 forks. Return it to the slow cooker.

7. Combine the cold water and ¼ cup more of flour in a container and stir until smooth. Slowly stir into the slow cooker and cook on low 15 more minutes so the stew thickens.

Slow Cooker Polish Kielbasa Stew

I love this recipe for cold nights. The Polish sausage melds well with the beans and tomatoes and the baby spinach gives it just the right thing. I like using cannellini beans, but they can be hard to find in dried version. Navy beans do just as well. Serve with crusty bread to make the meal complete.

Ingredients;
14 ounces of kielbasa, sliced in 1/2 inch coins
4 cups chicken broth
1 (14.5-oz) can of diced tomatoes, with the juice
1 pound dried white beans
1 large onion, peeled and chopped
1 teaspoon dried rosemary
1 cup water
6 cups baby spinach

Directions:

1. Prepare the slow cooker with nonstick spray.

2. Place the sliced kielbasa on the bottom of the slow cooker.

3. Pour the chicken broth and tomatoes on top.

4. Layer the dried beans next and top with onion and rosemary.

5. Add the water and cook low 7 to 8 hours or high 6 hours. Check the beans to make sure they are tender and cooked through.

6. Turn the slow cooker to high and cook 15 minutes. Add the baby spinach right before serving and let it wilt. Serve immediately.

Chapter 3: Slow Cooked Beef and Lamb Recipes That Make Your Mouth Water

The best part of using a Crock-Pot is that meat is cooked so slow and so long that it melts in your mouth. Use tougher cuts of meat that cost less and they will still come out savory and tender. Cook some beef stroganoff or a beef roast and how about a leg of lamb cooked in a Crock-Pot.

Asian-Inspired Beef and Broccoli

I usually get beef and broccoli whenever we go to a Chinese restaurant and although this isn't truly "Asian", it comes close. The best thing about this recipe is that you can change it with just two items. Switch out the beef for chicken strips cut from a chicken breast and use chicken broth rather than beef broth. Still use the brown sugar and everything else.

Ingredients:
1 tablespoon sesame oil
2 cloves garlic, peeled and minced
½ yellow onion, peeled and diced
1 – ½ pound beef chuck roast, sliced thin in 1-1/2-inch-long strips
1 cup beef broth
½ cup low sodium soy sauce
1/3 cup brown sugar, slightly packed
salt and pepper to taste
2-1/2 tablespoons cornstarch
3 cups fresh or frozen and thawed broccoli florets
sesame seeds

Directions:
1. Heat a skillet over medium high heat and add the sesame oil. Add the garlic and onions and sauté about 3 to 4 minutes. Add the beef and brown.

2. Prepare a Crock-Pot with a liner and pour the ingredients in the frying pan in. Make sure to scrape all the oil into the Crock-Pot.

3. Add the broth, soy sauce, brown sugar, salt and pepper.

4. Cook on low for 8 hours or on high for 4 hours.

5. Measure out ¼ cup of the liquid in the Crock-Pot into a small bowl or mug.

6. Add the cornstarch and mix well. Pour into the Crock-Pot along with the broccoli florets and stir. Cook another 20 minutes on high. The sauce should thicken.

7. Sprinkle with sesame seeds and serve over rice.

Corned Beef, Cabbage and Potatoes

I make this every St. Patrick's Day and it is so easy. The corned beef falls apart as you take it out of the Crock-Pot and it is very delicious.

Ingredients:
2 medium onions, peeled and sliced
1 to 2 cups whole baby carrots
6 medium red potatoes, quartered (do not peel)
1 (3 to 4 lb) corned beef brisket
1 bay leaf
1 can of beer
1 small cabbage, cut in wedges

Directions:
1. Prepare the Crock-Pot by spraying with nonstick spray.

2. Place the onions, baby carrots, and red potatoes on the bottom of the crock.

3. Trim some of the fat from the brisket and place it on top with the bay leaf on top of the brisket.

4. Pour the beer over top and cook low 8 to 9 hours.
5. During the last half hour of cooking, turn to high and place the cabbage wedges on top. They should be tender when removing.

6. Remove the cabbage and the brisket. Set the brisket aside for 5 minutes before slicing against the grain. Remove the vegetables with a slotted spoon, discard the bay leaf and serve.

Crock-Pot Braised Lamb Shanks

The sauce in this recipe is very tasty so serve with mashed potatoes or buttered noodles. You will want to get every drop.

Ingredients:
1 medium yellow onion, peeled and diced
2 carrots, peeled and diced
2 stalks of celery, diced
2 cloves of garlic, crushed
1 (14.5-oz) can crushed tomatoes
2 tablespoons tomato paste
1 bay leaf
1 teaspoon fresh thyme, chopped
2 cups chicken stock
4 lamb shanks, trimmed
Salt and pepper to taste
2 tablespoons olive oil
1 cup red wine

Directions:
1. Prepare the Crock-Pot by spraying with nonstick spray.

2. Place the onion, carrots, celery, garlic, crushed tomatoes and tomato paste in the bottom. Sprinkle the bay leaf and thyme over top.

3. Pour the stock in and stir gently.

4. Sprinkle salt and pepper to taste on the shanks.

5. Heat a skillet and add the olive oil. Brown the shanks over medium heat on all sides, about 5 minutes. Place shanks in the Crock-Pot.

6. Remove the skillet from heat and pour in the wine. Turn heat back on to medium high and bring to a simmer. Stir to get all brown bits up and pour into the Crock-Pot.

7. Cook on high 6 hours.

8. Remove the shanks and put them on a platter.

9. Remove the bay leaf and discard.

10. Use a stick blender on the sauce in the Crock-Pot and puree until it is smooth. Serve the sauce over the shanks and on some mashed potatoes or egg noodles.

Crock-Pot Meatloaf

In this recipe, you make 2 meat loaves and they will fit side by side in a large oblong Crock-Pot. Remember to use only 80% lean ground beef or you will have a Crock-Pot full of grease.

Ingredients:
1 tablespoon garlic powder
2/3 cup unseasoned bread crumbs
1/2 onion, peeled and diced
1/2 teaspoon salt
1 teaspoon pepper
1 teaspoon dried Italian seasoning herbs
2 eggs
1/2 cup milk
1-1/2 pounds ground beef
1 tablespoon Worcestershire Sauce
1 cup ketchup

Directions:
1. In a large bowl mix the garlic powder, bread crumbs, onion, salt, pepper and Italian herb seasoning. Add the eggs and milk and mix well with a fork.

2. Add the ground beef and mix well with the hands. Form into to loaves and put them in the bottom of a nonstick sprayed oblong Crock-Pot.

3. Whisk the Worcestershire sauce and ketchup in a 4-cup measuring cup until smooth and pour it over top of the meatloaves.

4. Cook on low for 8 to 10 hours. Remove from the crock and wait 5 minutes to slice and serve. They will be hard to get out intact, so it might be better to slice in the crock and pull the slices out with a spatula.

Italian Pot Roast

Want a little flair to your pot roast? This Italian-inspired recipe will be just the thing for you. Serve with a small side of pasta.

Ingredients:
1 teaspoon toasted, crushed fennel seed
1 teaspoon garlic powder
¼ teaspoon salt
1/2 teaspoon pepper
2-1/2 pound boneless beef pot roast
1 onion, peeled and cut thin
3 carrots, peeled and chopped
2 fennel bulbs, trimmed, cored and cut thin
1-(26-oz) jar tomato pasta sauce
1/4 cup fresh Italian parsley, chopped

Directions:
1. Toast the fennel seed by sprinkling on a foil covered baking pan sprayed with nonstick spray. Preheat broiler to high and put them in just long enough to toast them. Place in a mortar and pestle or in a grinder to grind coarsely.

2. In a small bowl, combine the fennel seeds, garlic powder, salt and pepper and set aside.

3. Trim the fat from the roast and rub with the herb blend on all sides. Wrap the roast in plastic wrap and place in the refrigerator overnight, if desired or continue with the recipe. (I just get everything ready and put the whole crock in the refrigerator to take out and turn on in the morning)

4. Prepare the Crock-Pot with nonstick spray and place the onions, carrots and sliced fennel in the bottom. Top with the roast.

5. Pour the tomato sauce over top.

6. Cook 9 to 10 hours on low or 5 hours on high.

7. Remove the roast and let it sit 5 minutes before slicing. Take the vegetables out with a slotted spoon and put in a bowl to serve with the roast.

8. Ladle out the remaining sauce to put over the roast, vegetables and a side of pasta.

Lamb Curry

I do not necessarily like Middle Eastern food, but this lamb is delicious. The recipe does have saffron in it, but it can be omitted. The cost of saffron is astronomical. The flavor is better with the saffron, but it is still good without it. Make basmati rice to serve with this dish.

Ingredients:
1 (14-oz) can of coconut milk
2 teaspoons coriander
1 teaspoon turmeric
1 tablespoon paprika
1/8 teaspoon saffron threads
1-1/2 teaspoons cumin
1-1/2 tablespoons fresh ginger, peeled and grated
1 (14-oz) can diced tomatoes
1/2 teaspoon salt
1 teaspoon pepper
2 tablespoons olive oil
3 cloves garlic, crushed
4 pounds lamb stew meat
Plain yogurt for garnish

Directions:
1. In a medium sauce pan, combine the coconut milk, coriander, turmeric, paprika, saffron, cumin and ginger. Cook over medium heat stirring occasionally, until it becomes smooth and creamy and it begins to steam but not boil. This will take about 5 minutes.

2. Prepare a Crock-Pot by spraying nonstick spray inside. Pour the hot coconut milk mixture in and add the diced tomatoes with juice, salt and pepper.

3. In a skillet, heat the olive oil and add the garlic. Sauté for 2 minutes and add the lamb meat to brown lightly on all sides. Place in the Crock-Pot and set low for 8 hours.

4. Take the lid off the Crock-Pot and place setting on high. Wait for half an hour to one hour. You want to let some of the liquid in the Crock-Pot evaporate so it thickens.

5. Serve over rice and top with some plain yogurt.

Leg of Lamb Off the Bone Crock-Pot Style

It might not be possible to cook a whole leg of lamb in a Crock-Pot, but this recipe comes as close to the flavor as any I have tasted. The meat is so tender you would swear it had a bone and it is so tender it just fell off. It would be impossible to fit a whole leg of lamb in so this the recipe calls for lamb shoulder that is cut in pieces.

Ingredients:
1 medium onion, peeled and chopped
1 cup baby carrots
2 cloves of garlic, peeled and chopped
1/2 cup halved dried apricots
1 teaspoon paprika
1 teaspoon ground cumin
1/2 teaspoon ground cinnamon
1/2 teaspoon ground ginger
2 tablespoons flour
1/4 teaspoon salt
1/2 teaspoon pepper
1-1/2 pound lamb shoulder
1/2 cup vegetable stock

Directions:
1. Prepare the Crock-Pot with nonstick spray.

2. Layer the onion, carrots, garlic and apricots on the bottom of the crock.

3. In a small bowl, combine the paprika, cumin, cinnamon, ginger, flour, salt and pepper. Whisk to mix and sprinkle over in the crock.

4. Trim any fat off the lamb and cut it in 1 inch pieces. Put on top in the crock.

5. Pour vegetable stock over the whole thing and cook low 8 hours or high 5 hours.

6. Whip up some couscous to serve with this dish. It will taste like leg of lamb.

Slow Cooked Salisbury Steak

Old fashioned Salisbury steak never tasted this good. It is so tender it is hard to believe. The gravy stews right in the crock. Always use lean ground beef when you cook it in a Crock-Pot or it will get very greasy because of the long cooking time. Never use less than 80% ground beef and it will be worth the cost.

Ingredients:
1/2 cup bread crumbs
1 egg
1/4 cup milk
1 teaspoon garlic powder
1 package onion soup mix
2 pounds ground beef
1 tablespoon butter
1 large sweet onion, sliced thin
3 tablespoons flour
1/4 cup beef broth
2 cans cream of mushroom soup

Directions:
1. In a large bowl mix the bread crumbs egg, milk garlic powder and soup mix. add the ground beef and combine by hand. Form into 8 patties and set aside on a plate.

2. Melt butter in a large skillet and sauté the onion until it is a little browned. Remove the onion with a slotted spoon and set aside.

3. Put the flour in a pie plate and slightly dredge the patties in it. Put them in the skillet and brown lightly on both sides. Place them in a slow cooker that has been prepared with nonstick spray.

4. Pour the onions on top of the patties

5. Whisk the beef broth and cream of mushroom soup in a large 4-cup measuring cup and pour over the onions and patties.

6. Cook on low for 6 hours and serve with mashed potatoes.

Slow Cooker Lamb Chops

Lamb chops are a favorite in my house and this is a favorite recipe. Sometimes you can stock up on lamb chops when they are on sale. You will want to get a bunch to keep in the freezer to make when you want something as delicious as this recipe.

Ingredients:
1 teaspoon garlic powder
1 teaspoon onion powder
1 teaspoon oregano
1/2 teaspoon thyme
1/4 teaspoon salt
1/8 teaspoon pepper
2 cloves garlic, peeled and minced
1 medium sweet onion, peeled and chopped
8 lamb chops

Directions:
1. In a small bowl, combine the garlic powder, onion powder, oregano, thyme, salt and pepper. Rub it into the lamb chops on both sides.

2. Prepare the slow cooker with nonstick spray and put the garlic and onions on the bottom. Place the lamb chops on top.

3. Cook 4 to 5 hours on low. Never do this on high. You can see there is little liquid in this recipe and if you cook on high, everything will dry out.

Slow Cooker Pepper Steak

This recipe will give you a little taste of Asia. It thickens right in the Crock-Pot and all you must do is prepare some rice to serve it over when you get home from work. I do not like to use bouillon, but it does make this recipe taste more flavorful. If you desire, omit the bouillon cube and use ¼ cup hot beef broth instead of water. Add 1-1/2 teaspoon of salt instead of just 1 teaspoon.

Ingredients:
3 Tablespoons vegetable oil
2 pounds beef sirloin, cut in 2-inch strips
1-1/2 teaspoons garlic powder
1 cube beef bouillon
¼ cup hot water
1 tablespoon cornstarch
2 green peppers, seeded and sliced thin
½ cup onion, peeled and sliced thin
1 (14.5-oz) can stewed tomatoes with the juice
3 tablespoons soy sauce
1 teaspoon salt
1 teaspoon sugar

Directions:
1. Place the vegetable oil in a skillet and heat.

2. Sprinkle the beef strips with the garlic powder and brown in the skillet. Transfer to the bottom of a slow cooker prepared with nonstick spray.

3. In a 4-cup measuring cup combine the bouillon cube and hot water until all is dissolved. Add the cornstarch and stir well. Pour into the slow cooker.

4. Layer the peppers, onions and tomatoes on top and sprinkle over the soy sauce, salt and sugar. Cook on high 3 to 4 hours or on low 6 to 8 hours.

Slow Cooker Stroganoff
Stroganoff is a staple for my family. They love the noodles and creamy beef and mushroom sauce and this recipe makes a lot of it. The only things you must do when you get home is add the mushrooms and cook the noodles. If you add the mushrooms at the beginning you will have mushroom mush. If you do not want to use the wine, increase the broth to 1 cup.

Ingredients:
1 – 1 pound round steak
1 teaspoon olive oil
2 tablespoons garlic, minced
1 medium sweet onion, peeled and sliced thin
1/2 teaspoon salt
1/2 teaspoon pepper
1 teaspoon dried parsley
1 teaspoon paprika
1/3 cup flour
3/4 cup beef broth
¼ cup sweet red wine
2 cups mushrooms, sliced
1 (8-oz) container of sour cream
2 cups cooked egg noodles

Directions:
1. With a sharp knife, remove the fat and cut the round steak in 1 inch diagonal strips.

2. Heat the oil in a large skillet and add the garlic. Sauté on medium heat for 2 minutes.

3. Add the steak strips and brown on all sides. Pour everything in the skillet into the bottom of a Crock-Pot that has been prepared with nonstick spray.

1. Cut the steak in diagonal strips and brown in a skillet with the olive oil and garlic. Place in the Crock-Pot that has been sprayed with nonstick spray.

2. Layer on the onions, salt, pepper and parsley.

3. Whisk the paprika, flour and beef broth in a 4-cup measuring cup until smooth and pour over top in the Crock-Pot.

4. Cook on low for 8 hours. During the last half hour add the mushrooms.

5. When ready to serve add the sour cream and stir in well. Cook 10 more minutes on high and ladle the mixture over hot egg noodles.

Vegetables and Eye of Round Roast
This is a good recipe for a tender eye of round roast and it is loaded with yummy vegetables. The flavor is simply delicious and your family will ask for it over and over. It is made with red potatoes, so the skins do not need to be peeled making it even easier to make.

Ingredients:
1 teaspoon garlic powder
1 teaspoon dried onion powder
1 teaspoon paprika
1 teaspoon oregano
1/2 teaspoon salt
1 teaspoon ground pepper
1 (3 to 4 pound) eye of round roast
1 whole onion, diced
2 stalks of celery, iced
3/4 cup baby carrots
6 to 8 red potatoes, quartered (do not remove skin)
1 (1.2-oz) package of dry beef gravy mix
1 tablespoon flour
1-1/2 cup beef broth

Directions:
1. Mix the garlic powder, onion powder, paprika, oregano, salt and pepper in a small bowl and rub this all over the roast. Don't waste any. If there is more in the bowl than you can put on the roast, add it to the flour when you use it. Set the roast aside. This is best done the night before wrapping the roast in plastic wrap and placing it in the refrigerator overnight.

2. Prepare the Crock-Pot with nonstick spray and place the onion, celery, carrots and potatoes in the bottom. Situate the roast on top.

3. Whisk the dry gravy mix, flour and beef broth in a glass 4-cup measuring cup until smooth and pour carefully over the roast.

4. Cook on high 5 hours or low for 8. Remove the roast and set it on a cutting board to rest for 5 minutes before slicing.

5. Remove the vegetables with a slotted spoon and place in a bowl.

6. The gravy should be thick, but if it needs a little more thickening, put another tablespoon of flour in, turn the Crock-Pot to high and whisk until smooth and thickened.

Chapter 4: Crock-Pot Pork and Chicken Recipes Fit For Royalty

I have never had a pork or chicken recipe that did not do well in a Crock-Pot. Pork comes out juicy and chicken is moist and flavorful. Make pork chops, ham, Chinese chicken and even chicken and biscuits in the Crock-Pot and they all will turn out like you are cooking for a king or queen.

Chicken Stew for Chicken and Biscuits
Traditional chicken and biscuits is stewed in a pot on the stove for a very long time. There is always a chance the chicken can scorch and when you make this in a Crock-Pot, that doesn't happen. This recipe does not indicate to use white or dark meat so just use what your family likes. The only thing you must do when you get home is make the biscuits.

Ingredients:
1 small yellow onion, peeled and chopped
2 stalks celery, sliced
1 cup baby carrots
3/4 cup flour
1/4 teaspoon parsley
1/8 teaspoon sage
1/8 teaspoon thyme
1/8 teaspoon rosemary
1/4 teaspoon salt
1/4 teaspoon pepper
1 – 1/2 pounds skinless chicken
1/2 cup white wine
1/2 cup chicken broth (or omit wine and use 1 cup chicken broth)
6 baking powder biscuits (make from dry biscuit mix and milk in the oven)
1 cup frozen peas
1/2 cup heavy cream
1/2 teaspoon more of salt
1/4 teaspoon more of pepper

Directions:

1. In a big bowl, place the onions, celery and carrots. Sprinkle over the flour and toss to coat.

2. Prepare a Crock-Pot with nonstick spray.

3. Place the vegetables in the bottom of the Crock-Pot.

4. In a small bowl, whisk together the parsley, sage, thyme, rosemary, salt and pepper and set aside.

5. Place the chicken in the Crock-Pot on top of the vegetables and sprinkle over the herb mixture.

6. Pour the wine and broth around the sides and cook on low 5 to 6 hours or on high about 3 hours.

7. About 15 minutes prior to being done, mix up baking powder biscuits and bake in the oven.

8. About 10 minutes prior to being done, pour the frozen peas in the Crock-Pot along with the additional salt and pepper. Stir and cook until finished.

9. Cut the biscuits in half, put the bottom in a bowl, pour the chicken mixture over top and top with the top of the biscuit to serve.

Chinese Inspired Cashew Chicken
I love cashew chicken from the Chinese restaurant in town. This isn't exactly like it, but it is a good substitute and it is so easy to make. I do not like canned mushrooms so I use a cup of regular mushrooms and sometimes I will use shitake mushrooms. Serve it with white or brown rice.

Ingredients:
2 – 1/2 teaspoons soy sauce
1 (10.75-oz) can of golden mushroom soup
2 teaspoons fresh shredded ginger
1/4 teaspoon salt
1/4 teaspoon pepper
1-1/2 pounds chicken tenders
1 (16-oz) package of frozen Asian vegetables (also called stir fry vegetables)

1 (4-oz) can sliced mushrooms, drained
3/4 cup whole or halved cashews
Cooked brown or white rice

Directions:
1. Prepare the Crock-Pot with nonstick spray.

2. Place the soy sauce and soup in the bottom and whisk together.

3. Add the ginger, salt and pepper and stir again.

4. Place the chicken in the Crock-Pot and layer on the vegetables that are still frozen and the drained mushrooms.

5. Cook on low 6 to 8 hours or on high 3 to 4 hours.

6. Right before serving, sprinkle the cashews over top and stir.

7. Serve over rice.

Company Slow Cooked Pork Roast with Sauerkraut and Kielbasa
We satisfy our pork and sauerkraut requirements on New Year's Day with this recipe. It is also good for sports parties and Oktoberfests. It is very meaty with both a pork loin and Polish sausage or kielbasa. I use either bagged or canned sauerkraut but like the bagged better because there is more liquid in it. I also like the fresh flavor of the bagged versus the canned.

Ingredients:
1/2 teaspoon salt
1/4 teaspoon pepper
2 tablespoons olive oil
1 – 2-pound boneless pork loin roast
3 sprigs of fresh thyme
4 pounds sauerkraut
1 pound kielbasa cut into coins (small pieces)

Directions:
1. Combine the salt and pepper and rub into the roast.

2. Heat a skillet on medium high heat and add the olive oil. Brown the roast on all sides and ends and set aside.

3. Prepare a slow cooker with nonstick spray and pour half of the sauerkraut in the bottom. Top with the browned roast with thyme sprigs on top.

4. Place the sliced kielbasa around the sides and cover with the rest of the sauerkraut.

5. Cook on high for 6 hours.

6. Remove roast and let sit 5 minutes before slicing. Remove rest of contents with a slotted spoon and serve in a bowl.

Crock-Pot Cola Ham
This recipe is made with soda. I like using coke. It gives a special flavor to the ham and makes it very tender and juicy.

Ingredients:
1 – 3 to 4 pound cooked boneless ham
½ cup brown sugar, packed
1 tablespoon prepared honey mustard
1 (12-oz) cans of cola

Directions:
1. Score the top and sides of the ham with diagonal diamonds.

2. In a bowl, make a paste with the brown sugar and mustard. Rube the paste into the scoring on the ham.

3. Prepare a Crock-Pot with nonstick spray and place the ham in the bottom.

4. Pour the cola along the sides of the Crock-Pot so you do not dislodge the paste.

5. Cook on low 7 to 8 hours.

6. Remove the ham from the Crock-Pot and let sit 10 minutes before slicing.

Crock-Pot Lemon Chicken
Citrus and chicken is always a delicious combination. The lemon flavor is milk and refreshing. Serve this at your next dinner party.

I do not use a whole chicken for this recipe because no one in my family likes dark meat. Instead, I use about 3 pounds of split, deboned chicken breasts.

Ingredients:
1 – 3-pound whole chicken (cut in pieces)
1/2 teaspoon salt
1/4 teaspoon pepper
2 tablespoons unsalted butter
2 cloves garlic, peeled and minced
1 teaspoon dried oregano that has been crumbled
3/4 teaspoon dried rosemary that has been crumbled
1/4 cup sherry or chicken broth
1/4 cup fresh squeezed lemon juice (about 2 to 3 lemons)

Directions:
1. Season the chicken pieces with salt and pepper.

2. In a skillet, melt the butter and add the garlic sautéing for 2 minutes over medium heat. Sprinkle the oregano and rosemary over the chicken.

3. Brown the chicken pieces and placing them in the bottom of nonstick sprayed Crock-Pot.

4. Add the sherry or broth to the skillet and scrape all the brown bits from the pan. Pour into the Crock-Pot.

5. Cook on low for 7 hours. Add the lemon juice and cook on low another hour or turn up to high and cook for 20 more minutes. Skim any fat from the juices and serve with the chicken.

Crock-Pot Pork Chops with Gravy
Make mashed potatoes or serve homemade coleslaw with these chops for a simple but delicious meal for the family or visitors.

Ingredients:
1/2 cup flour
1/2 teaspoon garlic powder
1/2 teaspoon dry ground mustard
1/2 teaspoon salt

1/4 teaspoon pepper
4 bone-in pork chops about 1/2 to 1 inch thick
2 tablespoons olive oil
1/4 cup more flour
1 (14.5-oz) can chicken broth

Directions:

1. In a re-closable plastic freezer bag, combine the ½ cup flour, garlic powder, dry mustard, salt and pepper and shake to mix it up.

2. Add a chop and shake to coat and remove to a plate. Do the same with the rest of the chops.

3. Heat a skillet over medium high heat and add the olive oil. Brown the chops on both sides.

4. Prepare the Crock-Pot with nonstick spray and place the chops on the bottom.

5. Pour have the broth around the chops. Reserve the rest.

6. Cook on low 3 to 4 hours. Do not overcook and do not cook on high because of the lack of liquid.

7. Remove the chops from the Crock-Pot and set aside to keep warm.

8. In a 4-cup measuring cup combine the ¼ cup flour and the rest of the chicken broth and whisk until smooth. Pour into the rest of the juice in the Crock-Pot and turn to high covering with the lid.

9. Cover and cook 10 minutes or until the gravy is thickened. Pour over the chops and mashed potatoes to serve.

Crock-Pot Roasted Whole Chicken
A large oblong Crock-Pot is required so you can fit a whole chicken in. If you love whole roasted chicken, you will love to make it this way all the time.

Ingredients:
1 large onion, peeled and cut into wedges
1/2 teaspoon garlic powder

1 teaspoon onion powder
1/4 teaspoon cayenne pepper
2 teaspoons paprika
1 teaspoon salt
1/4 teaspoon pepper
1 teaspoon dried thyme
1 – 4-pound whole chicken

Directions:

1. Prepare a Crock-Pot with nonstick spray.

2. Put the onion wedges in the bottom of the crock.

3. In a bowl, mix the garlic powder, onion powder, cayenne, paprika, salt, pepper and thyme. Mix well and set aside.

4. Remove the giblets from the chicken and rinse and dry the chicken with paper towels. Rub the outside and inside cavity with the herb mix. You can sauté the giblets and add to the Crock-Pot.

5. Place the chicken, breast down on top of the onions and cook 4 hours on low and 7 hours on high. Carefully remove the chicken and slice, but it will be so tender it might fall off the bone.

Ham Glazed with Maple and Brown Sugar
Get real maple syrup for this recipe because regular pancake syrup just doesn't do the trick. If you like pineapple, put some pineapple rings on top for a delicious feast.

Ingredients
1 – 5 to 6 pound fully cooked boneless ham
1/2 cup brown sugar, packed tight
1/2 cup prepared Honey Dijon mustard
1/2 cup maple syrup

Directions:

1. Prepare a Crock-Pot with nonstick spray.

2. Score the top of the ham by cutting a diamond pattern with a sharp knife and place the ham in the bottom of the Crock-Pot.

3. In a 4-cup measuring cup combine the brown sugar, honey Dijon mustard and maple syrup. Whisk until it is well blended and very thick. Pour over the ham and make sure to spread it so it glazes the entire top of the ham.

4. Cook on low 3 to 4 hours. Take a reading with a meat thermometer to read 140 degrees F.

5. Remove the ham and cover loosely with foil. Let it sit 15 minutes before slicing.

6. The juices in the Crock-Pot are too good to throw away, so strain them and serve with the juices over top ham slices.

Slow Cooked Non-Traditional Chicken Parmesan
In regular chicken Parmesan, the chicken is breaded and crispy. Crock-Pots don't do crispy very well, so this recipe is an "Untraditional" version. The crunch comes from breadcrumbs sprinkled over top instead of breading the chicken. It tastes much like the traditional type, but doesn't look like it. The chicken breast need to be thin for this recipe or it won't cook right. Take your chicken breasts and put them on a cutting board. Put your hand over top of the breast and press. Take a sharp knife and hold it parallel to the cutting board and slice under the hand – lengthwise. You will have a top and bottom.

Ingredients:
1 (8-oz) can tomato sauce
1 (28-oz) can crushed tomatoes with the juice
1 (3-oz) tomato paste
2 cloves garlic, peeled and crushed
2 whole chicken breasts, split and sliced – (4 halves cut in half for 8 pieces)
½ teaspoon salt
½ teaspoon pepper
1 tablespoon dried basil
2 cups mozzarella cheese, shredded
1 tablespoon olive oil
½ to ¾ cup breadcrumbs
Pinch of salt and pepper

1 tablespoon Parmesan cheese, grated

Directions:

1. Prepare a slow cooker with nonstick spray

2. Combine the tomato sauce, crushed tomatoes, tomato paste and garlic in the bottom of the slow cooker and stir.

3. Place sliced chicken breasts on top and sprinkle with ½ teaspoon each of salt and pepper.

4. Cook for 4 hours on high.

5. Remove the chicken from the Crock-Pot and add the dried basil and stir. Replace the chicken in the Crock-Pot.

6. Sprinkle the cheese over top and cover the Crock-Pot with the lid keeping it on high.

7. Heat a skillet over medium high heat and add the olive oil.

8. Pour in the bread crumbs and pinch of salt and pepper and stir constantly for 5 minutes. This will make the crumbs very crispy. Remove from the heat and add the parmesan. Set aside.

9. To serve, place some cooked pasta on a plate. Scoop out a chicken breast or two and put on top of the pasta. Pour a little sauce left at the bottom over top.

10. Top with breadcrumb mixture and serve.

Slow Cooked Pulled Pork

This pulled pork recipe is not only easy to make but it is better than most out there. The sauce is tangy and sweet and leaves a pleasant aftertaste. I like using the ginger ale in the recipe because it gives it a nice flavor. If you don't like ginger ale just use water, but try it once with it first to see if you like it.

Ingredients:
1 tablespoons light brown sugar
1/2 teaspoon cumin
2 teaspoons paprika
1 teaspoon dry mustard

1/4 teaspoon salt
1/4 teaspoon pepper
1 – 4-pound boneless pork shoulder, fat trimmed
2 teaspoons olive oil
3/4 cup water
3 tablespoons tomato paste
1/2 cup apple cider vinegar
2 more tablespoons brown sugar
1 can ginger ale plus enough water to make 2 cups
Your favorite barbecue sauce

Directions:

1. In a bowl, combine the 1 tablespoon brown sugar, cumin, paprika, dry mustard, salt and pepper and rub it all over the trimmed pork shoulder.

2. Heat a skillet on the stove over medium high heat and add the olive oil. Brown the shoulder on all sides. Place the pork on a plate.

3. Whisk ¾ cup water into the drippings in the skillet.

4. Prepare a slow cooker with nonstick spray and pour the juices inside.

5. Add the tomato paste, vinegar and 2 more tablespoons of brown sugar and mix the ingredients in the slow cooker well.

6. Measure the ginger ale into a measuring cup and add the water to make 2 cups. Pour this into the slow cooker.

7. Add the shoulder to the slow cooker and cook low 8 hours. This recipe does not do well on high as the flavors must be slow cooked.

8. Remove the pork from the slow cooker, cover with foil and set aside.

9. Strain the liquid in the slow cooker into a sauce pan and bring them to a boil. Cook until reduced by half, about 10 minutes after it starts to boil.

10. Place the pork shoulder on a cutting board and pull it apart with two forks. The slow cooking will have made it very

tender. Put the shredded pork in a serving bowl with 1 cup of the juice in the saucepan.

11. Serve the barbeque sauce on the side. Some people won't want it at all because this pulled pork is so flavorful, but if they do, you will have it handy.

.

Slow Cooker Chicken with Cranberries
Cranberry sauce is great with turkey but it is also very good with chicken. The cranberry sauce creates a glaze on this chicken recipe and makes everything delightfully sweet and sour. Use your favorite barbeque sauce for a flavorful meal. Use boneless chicken breasts if you like.

Ingredients:
2 tablespoons olive oil
1 medium yellow onion. Peeled and diced
4 chicken breast halves
1/2 teaspoon salt
1 cup barbecue sauce
1 (14-oz) can whole cranberry sauce
1/2 teaspoon ground ginger
1/2 teaspoon dried thyme
1/4 teaspoon pepper

Directions:
1. Prepare a slow cooker with nonstick spray.

2. Place a skillet on the stove over medium high heat and add the olive oil. Pour in the onions and sauté for about 2 minutes and remove to the bottom of the slow cooker.

3. Brown the chicken breasts on both sides in the skillet and place them on top of the onions in the slow cooker. Pour the barbecue sauce over topped with the cranberry sauce.

4. Sprinkle with the ground ginger, thyme and pepper.

5. Cook on low for 7 to 8 hours or on high 4 to 5 hours.

6. Remove the chicken breasts to a serving platter and ladle the sauce over top and serve.

Sunday Pork Roast with Gravy in a Crock-Pot

It might seem silly to season this roast with just one lonely whole clove, but it gives just enough spiciness to the dish. The roast comes out very tender and the gravy is ample and very flavorful. Put the roast on first thing in the morning and get dressed, put on makeup and pack lunches. It must be cooked on high for about 1 hour before being switched to low for 9 hours, so switch to low before you head out of the house.

Ingredients

1/2 teaspoon salt
1/4 teaspoon pepper
1 – 4 to 5-pound loin end roast
1 clove garlic, peeled and sliced
1 tablespoon olive oil
2 medium sweet onions, peeled and sliced thin
1 bay leaf
1 whole clove
1 cup hot water
2 tablespoons Worcestershire sauce
2 tablespoons cold water
2 tablespoons cornstarch

Directions:

1. Combine the salt and pepper and rub the roast with it. Cut slits in the top and insert garlic slices.

2. Heat a skillet over medium high heat and pour the olive oil into it. Brown the roast on all sides.

3. Prepare the Crock-Pot with nonstick spray and place half the sliced onions on the bottom. Layer on the roast and then the rest of the onions. Add the bay leaf to the top and insert the clove into the roast.

4. In a 4-cup measuring cup, mix the hot water with the Worcestershire sauce and pour around the sides of the pot and the roast. Cook on high for 1 hours and then reduce to low for 9 to 10 hours.

5. Remove the bay leaf and clove and discard. Remove the roast and let it sit for 5 minutes before slicing. Also take the onions out with a slotted spoon and put in a bowl.

6. In another bowl, mix the cold water with cornstarch to make a paste. Switch the Crock-Pot to high and whisk the paste into the juice. Replace the lid and turn to high. Once it comes to a boil, stir and the juice will thicken into gravy. It should only take about 15 minutes at the most.

Zesty Dijon Chicken
This is just so easy to make with a can of cream of mushroom soup, some cornstarch, chicken breasts and some seasoning. Throw it in and serve it with rice and noodles.

Ingredients:
4 to 6 boneless, skinless chicken breast halves
1 can cream of mushroom soup
2 tablespoons prepared Dijon mustard
¼ teaspoon black pepper

Directions:
1. Prepare a Crock-Pot with nonstick spray.

2. Place the chicken breasts in the bottom of the Crock-Pot.

3. In a bowl, combine the soup, mustard and pepper and whisk well. Pour over the chicken in the Crock-Pot.

4. Cook low 6 to 8 hours.

Chapter 5: Slow Cooker Seafood That Will Make You Drool

When you cook seafood in a Crock-Pot, you don't get that fishy smell that permeates the house. The smell is sealed in the Crock-Pot until it starts to cook and then it smells pretty good. It is possible to cook just about any type of seafood in a Crock-Pot like fish, shrimp, clams fish and even tuna noodle casserole.

Crab Legs Steamed in a Crock-Pot

I served this at our last Super Bowl party and it went over very well. You must use an oval Crock-Pot because the legs will not fit into a round one. Just leave the Crock-Pot hooked up on the buffet table because you don't have to worry about it drying out. You might start with 3 pounds of Crab legs, but trust me, you will want to double or even triple this recipe it is so good.

Ingredients:
3 pounds of Crab Legs
Water
1/2 stick of unsalted butter
1 teaspoon dried dill weed
4 cloves garlic, peeled and minced
Lemon and more melted butter for garnish

Directions:
1. You do not have to prepare the Crock-Pot because you are steaming the crab in water and nothing will stick.

2. Put the 3 pounds of rinsed crab legs in the Crock-Pot and put in enough water to cover them.

3. Cover and cook on high 4 hours. NOTE: If you use frozen crab legs, add ½ hour to the time.

4. Close to finishing time, melt the butter in a 4-cup measuring cup and mix in the dill and garlic.

5. Remove the crab legs from the Crock-Pot and serve with the melted butter mixture on the side.

Crock-Pot Creamy Salmon Hot Dish

I would use a liner when making this because even if you spray the Crock-Pot with nonstick spray it usually sticks. Take this to the church social because it is cheap to make since you use cans of flaked salmon.

Ingredients:
4 cups bread crumbs
3 (1 pound) cans of salmon drained
1 green pepper, seeded and chopped
1 (16 oz) can tomato puree
3 teaspoons fresh squeezed lemon juice
1 (14.5-oz) can cream of mushroom soup
6 beaten eggs
2 chicken bouillon cubes, crushed
1 can cream of celery soup
1/2 cup milk

Directions:
1. Place the liner in the Crock-Pot and spray with nonstick spray (It really sticks)

2. Put the bread crumbs in the bottom and put the flaked salmon on top.

3. In a bowl, combine the green pepper, tomato puree, lemon juice, mushroom soup. Beat the eggs in another bowl and add to the green pepper mixture sprinkling the crushed bouillon on top. Whisk well together and pour into the Crock-Pot over the salmon.

4. Cook on low 4 to 6 hours or high for 3 to 4 hours.

5. In a saucepan, whisk the milk with the celery soup over medium heat until it bubbles. Put this in a gravy boat.

6. The mixture in the Crock-Pot will be thick and like a casserole. Scoop it out and top with mixture in the gravy boat.

Crock-Pot Fish Tacos

Fish tacos are really popular these days and no wonder because they are good. This recipe calls for tilapia, but I do not like this fish. It is a bottom feeder and also called one of those garbage fish that eats anything on the sea floor. I use frozen white fish or cod to make my fish tacos and they are delicious.

Ingredients:
6 frozen tilapia fillets
1 (26-oz) can Ro-tel, drained
1/2 teaspoon garlic, minced
1/4 cup fresh cilantro, chopped
2 tablespoons fresh lime juice
1/2 teaspoon salt
1/4 teaspoon pepper
Soft Taco Shells, or hard if you prefer
Lettuce
Diced tomatoes
Salsa
Sour Cream

Directions:
1. Prepare the Crock-Pot with nonstick spray.

2. Place the fillets on the bottom and cover with the Ro-tel.

3. Add the garlic, cilantro, lime juice, salt and pepper.

4. Cook low for 4 hours. Flake the fish with a fork and mix in with the rest of the ingredients right before serving.

5. Spoon into taco shells and add lettuce, diced tomatoes, salsa and some sour cream.

.

Lobster Tail in a Crock-Pot

Yes, you can steam lobster tail in a Crock-Pot, but you need to have a wire rack that goes into the bottom and holds the tails about an inch above the bottom. This requires a large oval Crock-Pot so the tails can lay horizontally to steam.

Ingredients:
Water

¼ cup white wine
1 tablespoon sea salt
4 lobster tails
½ cup butter, melted

Directions:

1. Put the rack in the bottom of the Crock-Pot. There is no need to spray with nonstick spray because you are just steaming the tails.

2. Place about 1 inch of water in the bottom of the Crock-Pot. Add the white wine and sea salt.

3. Put the lid on and set to high. Watch for when the liquid starts to boil.

4. Once it boils, carefully put the lobster tails in the Crock-Pot using tongs. Be careful because you can burn yourself easily with the steam. Cover and steam 8 minutes. It is important that you do not lift the lid until this 8 minutes is up or you will release the steam that is cooking the lobster.

5. Remove the tails and serve with melted butter.

Louisiana Gumbo with Shrimp and Sausage

Gumbo is always fun to make and eat and this recipe gives you something of the Creole flavor from Louisiana. This recipe takes some time because much of it is prepared outside the Crock-Pot, but it is really good for parties. Once you are done, you leave it in the Crock-Pot and don't have to worry about it. You don't have to use a cast iron skillet, but for some strange reason, it makes the recipe taste better.

Ingredients:
1/2 cup flour
4 cloves of garlic, peeled and chopped
1 pound Andouille sausage, sliced in coins
1 yellow onion, peeled and chopped
1 green pepper, chopped
2 ribs of celery, chopped

1 (14.5-oz) can of diced tomatoes
3 bay leaves
2 teaspoons Creole seasoning mix
1/2 teaspoon thyme
4 cups chicken broth
3 pounds shrimp
Green onions for garnish
Italian Flat Leaf Parsley for garnish

Directions:
1. Begin by making a flour rue in the oven. Preheat the oven to 400 degrees F and sprinkle the flour in the cast iron skillet. Put it in the oven 5 minutes, stir and bake 5 to 10 minutes or until the four is brown. Remove from the oven and let cook at least 10 minutes before doing anything else.

2. In a Dutch oven, place the garlic and sausage and cook, stirring occasionally, over medium heat until brown. Drain on paper towels and place in the Crock-Pot that has been sprayed with nonstick spray.

3. To the Crock-Pot add the onion, peppers, celery, tomatoes, bay leaves, seasoning and thyme.

4. Whisk the flour mixture in the skillet with the chicken broth until smooth and pour it into the Crock-Pot.

5. Cook on high 6 hours.

6. Add the shrimp and cook on high 30 minutes. Stir once or twice during that time.

7. Remove the bay leaves and serve with a garnish of chopped green onions, and fresh parsley.

Old Faithful Tuna Noodle Casserole in a Crock-Pot
This traditional favorite does well in a Crock-Pot making it a good dish for that college student in a dorm room. Trouble is, that is smells good so most the students on the floor will want to visit when it is made. This recipe uses some sherry, but if that is not possible (some college students are under 21) just use 1/3 cup

chicken stock. The noodles do have to be cooked but that can be done in a microwave or on a hot plate. Don't cook them too long because they need to be al dente.

Ingredients:
10 ounces egg noodles, cooked and drained
2/3 cup milk
1/3 cup sherry
2 cans cream of celery or cream of mushroom soup
2 tablespoons dried parsley
2 cans tuna, drained well
2 tablespoons butter
10 ounces frozen peas

Directions:
1. Cook the egg noodles until still firm, drain and set aside until cool.

2. In a bowl, mix the milk, sherry or chicken stock, soup and parsley. Add the tuna and mix well again.

3. Prepare the Crock-Pot with nonstick spray.

4. Pour the ingredients in the bowl into the Crock-Pot and dot with the butter.

5. Cook on low 6 hours.

6. Add the peas and turn to high for 1 hour and serve hot.

Poached Salmon in a Slow Cooker
You can poach salmon in a slow cooker and it is much easier than doing it any other way. Serve this for guests and they will think you slaved over the stove for hours, but you didn't. Just start it up about 1 or 2 hours before dinner is served.

Ingredients:
2 cups water
1 cup dry white wine
1 thin sliced shallot
1 thin sliced lemon
1 bay leaf
2 sprigs dill

1 fresh tarragon sprig
2 sprigs fresh Italian parsley
1 teaspoon kosher salt
1 teaspoon black peppercorns, uncracked
4 to 6 salmon fillets with the skin on
Olive oil
More kosher salt
Lemon wedges

Directions:

1. You do not want to treat the Crock-Pot with nonstick spray or a liner in this recipe.

2. Place the water, wine, shallot, lemon, bay leaf and sprigs of herbs in the Crock-Pot.

3. Add salt and pepper.

4. Cover and cook on high ½ hour. It should be steaming when you are done.

5. Sprinkle the salmon with a pinch of salt and pepper and put in the hot water in the Crock-Pot with the skin side down.

6. Cover and cook low about 45 minutes. The salmon should become opaque and flake with a fork. It may take more than 45 minutes and you must watch it carefully. Once it is done you can serve immediately or turn the Crock-Pot to warm and leave it there 2 hours.

7. To serve, put the salmon on a serving plate, drizzle with olive oil and a little more salt. Serve thin lemon wedges on the side.

Seafood Feast in a Crock-Pot

If you love seafood, this is the dish for you because there is everything in it from shrimp to scallops to crab. This takes so little time to prepare, as long as you get peeled and deveined shrimp, you will have time to make dessert. Serve over rice or egg noodles for a feast you won't soon forget. Do not use frozen seafood because it adds too much liquid to the recipe.

Ingredients:
1 pound crab meat
1 pound bay scallops
1 pound peeled and deveined shrimp
2 (10.5-oz) cans of cream of celery soup
Milk – fill the 2 soup cans with milk to measure
2 tablespoons unsalted butter, softened
1 teaspoon Old Bay Seasoning
1/4 teaspoon salt
1/4 teaspoon pepper

Directions:
1. Prepare the Crock-Pot with nonstick spray

2. Layer in the crab, scallops and shrimp.

3. In a large bowl combine and whisk the soup and water until it is smooth. Pour it over the seafood in the pot.

4. Mix the butter with the seasonings. Use a fork to get it well incorporated and dot over the soup in the Crock-Pot.

5. Cook on low for 3 to 4 hours and serve over egg noodles or rice.

Shrimp Scampi Slow Cooker Style
Regular shrimp scamp can be a little tricky, but you won't have that problem with this recipe. You just layer everything in the slow cooker and set it. That is it. Do not use frozen shrimp because it adds too much liquid. I get raw peeled and deveined shrimp from the seafood store because I like eating shrimp, but hate preparing them. I tend to destroy the shrimp trying to get the vein out. It is worth it to me to get it done for me. It only takes a little over an hour to get a sumptuous seafood dinner on the table.

Ingredients:
1/4 cup chicken broth
1/2 cup white wine (or add a 1/2 cup more chicken broth)
2 tablespoons olive oil
2 tablespoons butter

2 tablespoons flat leaf Italian parsley, minced
1 tablespoon garlic, peeled and minced
1 tablespoon fresh squeezed lemon juice
1/2 teaspoon salt
1/4 teaspoon pepper
1 pound shrimp
Grated Parmesan cheese for garnish

Directions:

1. Place a liner in the Crock-Pot or spray with nonstick spray. The liner works better with this recipe simply because there is a great deal of liquid.

2. Pour the broth and wine in the bottom. Add the olive oil, butter, parsley, garlic, lemon juice, salt and pepper and stir.

3. Add the shrimp and cook for 1-1/2 hours on high or 2-1/2 hours on low. Serve with some grated Parmesan.

Shrimp with Rice

Use shrimp that has been deveined and then frozen to save time. I hate peeling and deveining shrimp and this ensures you already have clean shrimp. It is more expensive, but worth every penny.

Ingredients:
2 to 3 cloves of garlic, peeled and finely chopped
1 yellow onion, peeled and chopped
1 green bell pepper, seeded and chopped
1 red bell pepper, seeded and chopped
1 cup chicken broth
1 (10.5-oz) can cream of celery soup
1 (10.5-oz) can cream of chicken soup
1 (10-oz) can Ro-tel
2 cups uncooked instant rice
1 teaspoon dried parsley
1 – 1/2 pounds shrimp

Directions:
1. Prepare the Crock-Pot with nonstick spray.

2. Put the onion and both peppers in the bottom of the Crock-Pot.

3. Whisk the broth and both soups in a 4-cup measuring cup until it is smooth. Pour this over the vegetables.

4. Add the can of Ro-tel, the rice and parsley in the Crock-Pot.

5. Put the frozen shrimp on top.

6. Cook on low for 6 to 8 hours and serve.

Slow Cooked Clams with Tomato and Bacon
I think slow cookers were made just to do clams. When they are slow cooked the flavor is incredible. The clams are nice and tender and never get rubbery.

Ingredients:
6 thick cut slices of bacon
1/2 yellow onion, peeled and diced
1 (8-oz) bottle clam juice
1 (28-oz) can diced tomatoes, with juice
1 teaspoon dried oregano
3 tablespoon capers with the juice
2 dozen littleneck clams, cleaned.

Directions:
1. Slice the bacon in pieces that are 1 inch and fry in a skillet over medium heat. Drain on paper towels.

2. Place the onion in the skillet with the bacon grease and sauté for about 1 minute. Remove to a slow cooker that has been prepared with nonstick spray.

3. Cut the bacon in 1 inch pieces and fry in a skillet. Drain on paper towels.

4. Cook the diced onion in the bacon drippings for about 1 minute.

5. Place the onions in the bottom of the slow cooker and slowly pour the clam juice in.

6. Add the tomatoes, oregano and capers and cook on low for 3 to 4 hours.

7. 1 hour before you want to serve, turn up the Crock-Pot to high. Wait 15 minutes and pour in the clams. Cook 30 to 40 more minutes but do not lift the lid. You are steaming the clams and if you open it the clams will never open. Watch through the glass to make sure they open and when they do, the dish is ready to serve. Get rid of any clams that do not open.

8. I serve my clams with a little spaghetti and red sauce.

Slow Cooker Mussels in Tomato Basil Sauce
This dish will get you salivating while it is cooking. It is very easy to make and only takes about 4 to 5 hours, but you can keep it going longer. I use fresh basil from my garden and pick a big handful of leaves to chop. I put most of them in the Crock-Pot but keep a few chopped leaves out to sprinkle on top of each plateful too.

Ingredients:
2 tablespoons butter
1 (6-oz) can tomato paste
1 onion, peeled and chopped
2 cloves garlic, peeled and chopped
2 (14.5-oz) cans diced tomatoes, drained
Handful of fresh basil leaves, chopped
½ teaspoon salt
½ teaspoon pepper
1 cup white wine

Directions:
1. In a skillet, over medium high heat, melt the butter. Once melted add the tomato paste and stir into a paste. Add the onion and garlic and sauté, stirring for 1 to 2 minutes.

2. Reserve about 2 tablespoons of the chopped basil for garnish for garnish. Set aside.

3. Add the diced tomatoes that have been drained (too much fluid) and half the basil. Stir and bring to a simmer. Simmer 2 minutes.

4. Prepare a slow cooker with nonstick spray.

5. Place rinsed mussels in the bottom of the Crock-Pot. Pour the sauce in the skillet over. Put the rest of the basil on top and season with the salt and pepper.

6. Add the wine and cook on low 4 to 5 hours. Stir and make sure all the mussels open before serving. Discard those that do not.

7. Serve in bowls with more basil sprinkled over each bowl.

Chapter 6: Crock-Pot Pasta, Rice and Grain Recipes to Die For

Pasta dishes come out surprisingly good in a Crock-Pot. So do rice and other grain recipes. They are rarely over cooked and slimy and are usually cooked to perfection. Make macaroni and cheese, lasagna, rice dishes and more.

Cheese and Chicken Pasta

This is sort of like creamy macaroni and cheese with spaghetti pasta and chicken. The sauce is very creamy due to using a combination of cream cheese and cheddar. The pasta is put in dry and cooks during the regular cooking time with no need to boil it outside the Crock-Pot. One word of warning. If your chicken breasts are thick you must cut them in half lengthwise to make 2 pieces. This will ensure no one will get a raw piece of chicken.

Ingredients:
1 pound boneless, skinless chicken breasts
3 cups chicken broth
2 cloves garlic, peeled and minced
2 tablespoons onion, chopped green
1/4 teaspoon salt
1/4 teaspoon pepper
1 (16-oz) package uncooked spaghetti
2 cups shredded mild Cheddar cheese
1 (8-oz) package cream cheese

Directions:
1. Prepare a slow cooker with nonstick spray.

2. Place the chicken in the bottom and add the chicken broth, garlic, onion, salt and pepper.

3. Cook on high 4 hours or on low 7 to 8 hours.

4. Take the chicken out and shred it with two forks on a cutting board. Return it to the slow cooker.

5. Break the dry spaghetti in half and place in the slow cooker.

6. Add the shredded cheese and cut the cream cheese in small chunks and place on top. Give it a good stir. (If the combination looks dry and thick, add ½ cup of water so the spaghetti will cook).

7. Cook on high 30 minutes or until the pasta is tender enough to eat.

8. Stir to combine completely and serve.

Cheesy Tortellini in a Crock-Pot
Tortellini is a pasta with cheese or meat inside, twisted into a little "O". For this recipe use the cheese type, but you can always try the meat variety for a change. Use the pasta frozen so it adds a little moisture to the Crock-Pot. You decide if you want to use mild, sweet or hot Italian sausage.

Ingredients:
1 tablespoon olive oil
1 clove garlic, peeled and minced
1 small yellow onion, peeled and chopped
1 pound bulk Italian Sausage
1 (14-oz) can diced tomatoes with the juice
1 (26-oz) jar pasta sauce
1 teaspoon Italian seasoning
1 (16-oz) package cheese tortellini
1-1/2 cups shredded Mozzarella cheese
¼ cup grated Parmesan cheese

Directions:
1. Put a skillet on the stove over medium high heat and add the olive oil.

2. Add the garlic and onion and sauté for about 3 minutes.

3. Add the sausage and stir constantly until the sausage has browned. Drain well.

4. Prepare a Crock-Pot with nonstick spray and pour the sausage mixture in the bottom.

5. Layer in the can of tomatoes with juice and pasta sauce and sprinkle the Italian seasoning over top. Stir well.

6. Cook on low for 7 to 8 hours.

7. Stir in the frozen tortellini and turn to high. Cook about 20 to 40 minutes or until the tortellini is tender and hot all the way through. Turn the Crock-Pot off.

8. In a bowl, combine the two cheeses and sprinkle over top of the ingredients in the Crock-Pot. Put the lid back on and wait about 5 minutes until the cheese melts. Serve immediately.

Chicken and Broccoli in Couscous

Couscous is another grain that wasn't around much until recently. It comes from North Africa and to my surprise isn't really a grain. It is made of grains including semolina and wheat that has been steamed. Pearl, or Israeli couscous, looks like little balls that have a nutty flavor and chewy consistency. Plain couscous looks a bit like rice and cooks up in minutes to a fluffy texture. I personally like regular couscous and use it in main dishes and in cold salads with fruit and vegetables. This is a main dish with chicken and broccoli.

Ingredients:
2 pounds skinless, boneless chicken breasts cut in 2 inch pieces
2 cups chicken broth
1/2 teaspoon salt
1/4 teaspoon pepper
2 cloves garlic, peeled and minced
2 cups frozen broccoli florets
1 cup plain couscous

Directions:
1. Prepare the Crock-Pot with nonstick spray.

2. Put the chicken pieces on the bottom of the Crock-Pot.

3. Pour the broth around the sides of the Crock-Pot.

4. Sprinkle over the salt pepper and garlic and give it a stir.

5. Cook on low 6 hours or high for 3 hours.

6. Add the broccoli (do not thaw) and cook 30 more minutes covered, on high.

7. Turn the Crock-Pot off and add the couscous. Stir to combine all the ingredients and put the lid back on. Leave alone for 10 minutes and fluff with a fork before serving.

Crock-Pot Quinoa

A few years ago, no one even heard of quinoa in my neck of the woods. Now it is on practically every grocery store shelf and in most pantries. This grain is very nutritious and delicious. It comes from the Andes Mountains and is filled with protein making it very filling. It is very easy to digest and is considered a 'superfood'. There are a lot of good things in this recipe including more protein from beans and many different vegetables. It is healthy, but it is also good and even the kids will like it.

Ingredients:
1 tablespoon olive oil
3 cloves garlic, peeled and minced
1 cup yellow onion, peeled and chopped
1-1/2 cups bell pepper (any color), seeded and chopped
1-1/2 cup dry quinoa
1 (8-oz) can of tomato sauce
1 (14.5-oz) can tomatoes with green chilies, undrained
2-1/2 cups vegetable broth
1-1/2 teaspoon cumin
1/2 teaspoon salt
1/4 teaspoon pepper
1 (14.5-oz) can pinto beans, drained and rinsed
1 (14.5-oz) can black beans, drained and rinsed
1-1/2 cups frozen corn kernels
1-1/2 cups shredded Monterey Jack or Cheddar cheese
1 avocado, diced
3 to 4 Roma tomatoes, diced
1/2 cup cilantro, chopped
1/2 cup green onion, chopped
1 lime cut in wedges

Directions:

1. Put a skillet on the stove and add the olive oil.

2. Sauté the garlic, onion and bell pepper about 3 to 4 minutes.

3. Prepare a Crock-Pot with nonstick spray and put the garlic mixture in the bottom.

4. Add the quinoa, tomato sauce, undrained tomatoes, broth, cumin, salt and pepper and mix.

5. Cook on high 3 hours. You might want to look to make sure it isn't drying out and if it is, add a little water.

6. Add the beans and frozen corn (do not thaw) and stir. Sprinkle the cheese on top and cover cooking on high 15 more minutes.

7. Serve by putting the avocado, tomatoes, cilantro, green onion and limes in little bowls. Let family and guests add what they want to a big scoop of quinoa in a bowl.

Crock-Pot Stuffed Manicotti

Use Manicotti, also called sewer pipes, or large pasta shells to make this delicious dish. Again, this one has green stuff in it, but you can omit it if you like. One person in my family is a purist and does not like spinach in his stuffed pasta. I make his manicotti first and then cut the spinach in half and use the other half for a vegetable for another dinner. Do not cook the manicotti first. Instead, stuff it dry and put it in the Crock-Pot. It will soften while it cooks.

Ingredients:
1 (15-oz) container ricotta cheese
1 (10-oz) package of frozen spinach, thawed and squeezed dry as possible
1 slightly beaten egg
1/2 cup shredded mozzarella cheese
1/2 cup grated Parmesan cheese, divided
1/4 teaspoon salt
1/4 teaspoon pepper

2 (14.5-oz) cans stewed tomatoes
1 (24-oz) jar pasta sauce, divided
1 (8-oz) package of dried Manicotti shells
1/2 teaspoon dried basil
1 clove garlic, minced
1 teaspoon dried oregano

Directions:

1. In a bowl, combine the ricotta, spinach, egg, ¼ cup of the Parmesan cheese, the mozzarella cheese, salt and pepper. Mix it well and set it aside.

2. In another bowl, whisk one can of tomatoes with the 1 cup of the pasta sauce.

3. Put a liner in the Crock-Pot and place the tomato sauce mixture in the bottom.

4. Stuff the cheese mixture into the dry Manicotti shells using your fingers, and be careful not to stuff them so full they break. Put a layer of the stuffed Manicotti on top of the tomato mixture in the Crock-Pot. You won't use them all.

5. Combine the rest of the pasta sauce and the other can of tomatoes in the same bowl and add the basil, garlic and oregano. Whisk well and pour half over top of the Manicotti.

6. Put another layer of Manicotti in the pot and this time you should use them all.

7. Cover with the rest of the sauce and sprinkle on the rest of the Parmesan cheese.

8. Cook 3 to 4 hours and serve.

Delectable Macaroni and Cheese in a Crock-Pot
The family loves this dish and we serve it at parties by making a macaroni and cheese bar. We fry up bacon, cook some ham, chop green onions, supply hot sauce and more. Guests go down the line and get a bowlful out of the Crock-Pot and mix in whatever they want. When you cook the macaroni leave it even harder than al dente. If you don't, it will be very mushy. Cook it until you

can bite it without it crunching, but it is still too hard to comfortably eat. Some of these recipes have the pasta put right in the Crock-Pot with everything else and in others, the pasta is boiled as usual and the Crock-Pot ingredients are served over top or the cooked pasta is put in right before serving. Make sure you pay close attention to the directions.

Ingredients:
4 cups dried elbow macaroni
2 cups milk
6 tablespoons butter, sliced in small pieces
1 cup sour cream
4 cups shredded sharp Cheddar cheese, divided
2 (14.5-OZ) cans Cheddar cheese soup
3/4 teaspoon dry mustard or 3/4 teaspoon hot sauce
1/2 teaspoon salt
1/2 teaspoon pepper

Directions:
1. In a Dutch oven, boil a pan full of water and add the macaroni. Boil no longer than 6 to 8 minutes testing after 6 minutes.

2. Prepare the Crock-Pot with a liner. A liner works better for this recipe because it does tend to stick.

3. Place the milk, butter, sour cream and 3 cups of the cheese, soup, mustard or hot sauce and salt and pepper in the Crock-Pot and mix it up.

4. Cook on low for 20 to 30 minutes. Stir to mix in the butter that has melted.

5. Cook 2 to 3 hours until the edges turn a light brown. Add the remaining cheese and cook 15 more minutes until it melts and serve.

Easy Tender Ravioli in a Crock-Pot
This recipe is super easy and delicious. Layer frozen ravioli, sauce and cheese in the Crock-Pot and cook while at work. Serve with a salad and crusty bread for a delicious meal.

Ingredients;
1 tablespoon olive oil
1 clove garlic, peeled and minced
1 medium sweet onion, peeled and chopped
2 (26-oz) jars of four cheese tomato pasta sauce
1 (15-oz) can of tomato sauce
1-1/2 teaspoon dried Italian seasonings
1/4 teaspoon salt
2 (25-oz) package of frozen ravioli
2 cups shredded mozzarella cheese
1/4 cup fresh chopped flat leaf parsley

Directions:

1. Place a skillet on the stove over medium heat and pour in the olive oil. Sauté the garlic and onion for about 5 minutes or until tender.

2. Add the pasta sauce and tomato sauce with Italian seasoning and salt and stir to combine well.

3. Use a liner to protect the Crock-Pot.

4. Measure out 1 cup of the sauce mixture and place it in the bottom of the Crock-Pot.

5. Add one package of the frozen ravioli (it must be frozen still – do not thaw). Sprinkle 1 cup of the mozzarella on top.

6. Place the second bag of frozen ravioli on top with the rest of the cheese. Pour the rest of the sauce over top.

7. Cook on low for 5 to 6 – ½ hours.

8. Garnish with chopped parsley before serving.

Risotto Cooked in a Crock-Pot

Risotto is one of those things many people avoid making because they think it is difficult to get right. I have had some epic failures in the risotto area myself, but when you cook it in a Crock-Pot, very little can go wrong. Do not use anything but risotto rice, also called Arborio rice. Other rice does not stand up to the standards of risotto and will either come out crunch or mushy. If you do not want to use the wine, just add ¼ cup more chicken broth or water. Use a liner in your Crock-Pot or you might have a mess to clean up later.

Ingredients:
1-1/4 cup uncooked Arborio rice
1/4 cup olive oil
4 cloves of garlic, peeled and minced
1 teaspoon dried onion flakes
1/2 teaspoon salt
1/4 teaspoon pepper
3-1/2 cups chicken broth
1/4 cup dry white wine
1 cup grated Parmesan cheese (not out of the shaker box – the real thing)

Directions:
1. Place a liner in the Crock-Pot.

2. Pour the dry, uncooked rice in the bottom of the Crock-Pot with the olive oil. Stir it around to make sure that the rice is coated with the oil.

3. Add the garlic, onion flakes, salt and pepper.

4. Pour the chicken broth and wine around the sides of the Crock-Pot.

5. Cook on high for 2 hours. Test the rice to make sure it is tender before proceeding.

6. Add the grated cheese and stir in. Turn off the Crock-Pot and let the risotto sit 15 minutes without the lid on so the steam escapes. Stir and serve.

Slow Cooked Red Beans and Rice
I am not Hispanic but have friends that are. The beans and rice made by Aunt Antonella, one of my high school friend's aunts, were the best I've ever tasted, hands down. She made them the old way. My slow cooker beans and rice isn't bad, but it isn't as good as Aunt Antonella's, but it is close. This is one of those meals you make right before payday because the ingredients are

inexpensive and the dish goes a long way to filling you up. Use dried kidney beans as they will cook soft in the slow cooker. I use Andouille sausage, but even kielbasa is good in this recipe. Sometimes I don't put it in at all, depending on if I am using this as a side dish or not.

Ingredients:
2 cups dried red kidney beans
4 cloves garlic, peeled and minced
1 -1/2 cup yellow onion, peeled and chopped
1-1/2 cups red bell pepper, seeded and chopped
1-1/4 cup celery, chopped
1 teaspoon ground red pepper flakes
2 teaspoons paprika
1-1/2 teaspoon dried thyme
1/2 teaspoon black pepper
1/2 teaspoon salt
2 bay leaves
1 (1 pound) package of sausage, sliced
3 cups vegetable broth
3 cups water
5 cups cooked long grain rice
3/4 cup green onions, chopped

Directions:
1. Prepare the slow cooker with non-stick spray or use a liner.

2. Place the dry kidney beans in the bottom of the crock with the garlic, onion, pepper, celery, red pepper flakes, paprika, thyme, pepper, salt and by leaves.

3. Spray the slow cooker with nonstick spray and combine the beans, onion, peppers, celery, garlic, thyme, red pepper flakes, black pepper, salt and bay leaves in the bottom.

4. Place the sliced sausage on top and add the broth and water along the sides of the Crock-Pot. Don't mix.

5. Cook on high 5 hours. Check the tenderness of the beans. Sometimes it takes a little longer for them to cook.

6. While the beans are cooking, make the rice. I put some rice in an individual serving bowl and ladle bean sauce over top sprinkling with some green onions before serving.

Slow Cooker Lasagna

In this recipe, the dry noodles are put in the slow cooker and you must watch because they tend to break when you make them fit into the curves of an oval Crock-Pot. I have soaked my lasagna noodles in warm water for about 10 minutes and then put them in. You just must reduce the amount of time you cook by about 15 minutes to a half hour when you do that. This recipe uses Swiss chard and that tastes fantastic in it. If you don't like vegetables in your lasagna just omit it. It is also possible to use baby spinach if Swiss chard is not readily available.

Ingredients:
2 (28-oz) cans of diced tomatoes with juice
3 cloves of garlic, peeled and chopped
1 (16-oz) container Ricotta cheese
1/2 cup flat leaf parsley, chopped
1/2 cup grated Parmesan cheese
1/4 teaspoon salt
1/4 teaspoon pepper
1 (12-oz) package of dry lasagna noodles
1 bunch Swiss chard, torn into small pieces
1 (12-oz) package of shredded mozzarella cheese

Directions:
1. In a bowl, mix the diced tomatoes with juice and the garlic.

2. In another bowl combine the Ricotta, parsley, Parmesan, salt and pepper and mix.

3. Prepare a Crock-Pot with a liner.

4. Place enough of the tomato mixture in the bottom to cover and place a layer of lasagna noodles to fit on the bottom.

5. Make a layer of Swiss chard with 1/3 of the Ricotta mixture dropped in dollops on top.

85

6. Spread a layer of tomato sauce on top with some more mozzarella.

7. Layer another set of noodles on top and keep layering with ricotta, sauce, cheese, chard and so on ending with cheese.

8. Cook low for 2 to 3 hours or until the noodles are tender and not gummy.

Slow Cooker Spanish Rice with Flair

Spanish rice is normally spicy and flavorful and this dish is no exception. It uses chili powder and cumin to give it the flair Spanish rice should have. I also add in black beans to make it a complete meal. Omit those if you just want to use as a side dish.

Ingredients:
2 T olive oil
2 cups raw Jasmine rice
1 medium yellow onion, peeled and chopped
1 (14-oz) can diced tomatoes with the juice
2 cups chicken stock
3 cloves garlic, peeled and minced
1 red bell pepper, seeded and chopped
2 teaspoons chili powder
1-1/2 teaspoon cumin
½ teaspoon salt
1 (15.5-oz) can black beans, rinsed and drained
Sour cream
Chopped fresh cilantro

Directions:
1. Put a skillet on the stove over medium high heat and add the olive oil.

2. Pour the raw rice in and sauté until all rice is coated with olive oil.

3. Add the onion and sauté until the rice is a light golden brown, about 5 minutes.

4. Prepare the slow cooker with nonstick spray and pour in the rice mixture.

5. Add the tomatoes with the juice, chicken stock, garlic, bell pepper, chili powder, cumin and salt and mix.

6. Cook on high 2-1/2 hours to 3 hours. Check after 2 to make sure the rice isn't drying out. If so, add a little water.

7. The last 20 minutes of cooking, add the rinsed and drained black beans and stir in.

8. Serve with a dollop of sour cream and sprinkle some chopped cilantro over top.

Slow Cooker Spirals with Italian Sausage and Peppers
The scent from this dish is reminiscent of fair sausage and pepper sandwiches and it is best to make it when you are out of the house. It starts to waft fragrance after about an hour and you must wait 3 more to eat it. The recipe calls for green and red bell peppers, but use any combination or colors of bell pepper as long as you use three of them. Substitute mild sausage for hot if you can't stand the heat.

Ingredients:
1 teaspoon olive oil
1 clove garlic, peeled and minced
1 large sweet onion, peeled and sliced thin
1 pound sweet Italian sausage
1 pound hot Italian sausage
2 green bell peppers, seeded and sliced in strips
1 red bell pepper, seeded and sliced in strips
1 (24-oz) jar of your favorite pasta sauce
Salt and pepper to taste
1 (16-oz) package of spiral pasta or macaroni

Directions:
1. Place a skillet over medium high heat and add the olive oil. Sauté the garlic and onion until tender, about 3 to 5 minutes.

2. Put both types of sausage in the skillet and brown. Drain any grease.

3. Prepare a Crock-Pot with nonstick spray and add the sausage mixture to the Crock-Pot. Add the peppers, sauce, salt and pepper.

4. Cook on high 3 to 4 hours.

5. Right before serving cook up the pasta per the package instructions until al dente and drain. Serve the sausage and pepper mixture over top the pasta.

Chapter 7: Delicious Vegetarian Dishes that Everyone Loves

I am not a vegetarian but have a few friends that are. I have found that I really like some vegetarian dishes and I bet your family will too if you try some of these in this chapter. The Rice and beans are especially delicious and the stuffed peppers are really good. You won't miss the meat in these recipes.

Brussels Sprouts in Balsamic Sauce
Get ready for a flavor explosion in your mouth with this dish. Vegetarians can use this as a main dish, or you can make it as a side dish for those that aren't vegetarian. Either way, family and guests alike will love Brussels sprouts even if they didn't like them before.

Ingredients:
2 tablespoons brown sugar, packed
½ cup Balsamic vinegar
2 pounds fresh Brussels sprouts, trimmed and halved
2 tablespoons olive oil
Kosher salt and cracked pepper to taste
2 tablespoons unsalted butter
¼ cup Parmesan, fresh grated

Directions:
1. In a saucepan, combine the brown sugar and vinegar. Mix well over medium heat and bring to a light boil. Reduce the sauce by half. This will take about 6 to 8 minutes over a light boil. Set the saucepan aside to cool.

2. Prepare a slow cooker with nonstick spray.

3. Put the sprouts in the bottom.

4. Add the salt and pepper and dot with the unsalted butter.

5. Cook on low for 3 to 4 hours or on high 1 to 2 hours.

6. Drizzle with the Balsamic sauce, sprinkle with cheese and serve immediately.

Cauliflower Bolognese

You never knew that cauliflower could taste so good. This Bolognese sauce is served over egg noodles or you can substitute whole wheat noodles. It doesn't taste like meat sauce and has its own unique flavor. The recipe calls for fire roasted tomatoes in a can, and they can be hard to find. Just use a regular can of tomatoes and it will taste fine.

Ingredients:
1 fresh head of cauliflower
2 cloves garlic, minced
1 cup red onion, peeled and diced
1 teaspoon dried basil
2 teaspoons dried oregano
1/2 cup vegetable broth
2 (14-oz) cans of fire-roasted diced tomatoes
1/4 teaspoon red pepper flakes
1/4 teaspoon salt
1/4 teaspoon pepper

Directions:
1. Cut the head of cauliflower into small florets.

2. Prepare a Crock-Pot with nonstick spray.

3. Place the cauliflower florets on the bottom of the Crock-Pot.

4. Add the garlic, onion, basil, oregano, broth, tomatoes, red pepper flakes, salt and pepper. Do not mix.

5. Cook on high for 5 hours.

6. Give the cauliflower a bit of a mash with a potato masher or fork before serving over noodles.

Cheesy Bean and Rice Casserole Slow Cooker Style

Want to fix something easy to cook for dinner on a Saturday afternoon. This is the dish and it is a favorite of my family. The recipe calls for black-eyed peas, but you can use pinto, Great Northern or any other type of bean instead. Cook rice the night before so it can cool. It won't be mushy if you do and this aids the black-eyed peas or beans to soak up most of the water in order to be tender. The spices might be a little heavy for some, but you can always cut down on the amount you put in.

Ingredients:
1 – 1/2 cups dried black-eyed peas
2 cloves garlic, peeled and chopped
1 red bell pepper, seeded and diced
1 medium yellow onion, peeled and diced
1 (28-oz) can of diced tomatoes with juices
1 (10-oz) can corn, drained
2 teaspoons cumin
1/4 cup chili powder
2 cups rice, cooked and cooled
1/2 to 1 cup shredded Cheddar

Directions:
1. Drain and rinse the black-eyed peas.

2. Prepare the slow cooker with nonstick spray.

3. Place the black-eyed peas in the bottom of the slow cooker.

4. Add the garlic, bell pepper, onion, tomatoes and corn. Stir and cook on high for 2 hours.

5. Add the cumin and chili powder and stir. Pour in the cooked and cooled rice and the cheese cooking 30 more minutes.

6. Serve with a dollop of sour cream.

Crunchy White Bean Chili
You might wonder how crunchy chili could be any good. The crunch comes from corn chips and it gives extra dimension to this dish.

Ingredients:
3 cups onion, peeled and chopped, divided
3 garlic cloves
3 cups red or green bell pepper, chopped

1 tablespoon dry oregano
1/2 cup fresh chopped cilantro
3 dried ancho chilies
1/4 cup olive oil
2 tablespoons tomato paste
1/2 tablespoon ground cumin
1/2 teaspoon coriander
1 teaspoon kosher salt
1 teaspoon pepper
1 bay leaf
1 (26-oz) can tomato puree
4 – 1/2 cups vegetarian vegetable stock
1 (16-oz) package of dried white beans
4 cups zucchini, peeled and diced
1 (15-oz) can diced tomatoes
Sour cream
Corn chips

Directions:

1. In a blender or food processor, place 1 cup of the onion, garlic cloves, 1 cup of the bell pepper, oregano and cilantro. Process a few pulses.

2. Remove the stems and seeds from the ancho chilies and chop slightly. Add to the blender or food processor and process until almost smooth.

3. Put a large skillet over medium heat and add the olive oil and pour in the mixture in the blender or processor. Cook, stirring frequently for 8 minutes. Some of the liquid should start to evaporate.

4. Add tomato paste, cumin, coriander, salt, pepper and bay leaf. Stir constantly another 2 minutes.

5. Prepare a Crock-Pot with nonstick spray.

6. Pour the mixture in the skillet into the Crock-Pot. Mix in the rest of the onions, 1 cup of the bell pepper (set the rest aside), tomato puree, vegetable stock and beans. Stir and cook on low for 8 hours.

7. Switch to high and add the remaining bell peppers, zucchini, and diced tomatoes. Cook on high 20 more minutes.

8. When ready to serve, pull out the bay leaf and ladle the chili in bowls. Top with sour cream and a handful of crushed corn chips.

Curried Couscous Vegetables

I normally do not like curry, but this dish is delicious. It might be a little strong for some so you can cut down on some of the spices if you desire. Try it once with the full strength, especially if you have a cold. You WILL be able to taste it. The yogurt brings on a cooling sensation when the dish is eaten.

Ingredients:
4 cups potatoes, peeled and diced
1 cup yellow onion, peeled and chopped
3 cloves peeled garlic, minced
1 cup carrot, peeled and chopped
4 cups tomato, chopped
1 green bell pepper, seeded and cut into strips
1 teaspoon salt
2 tablespoons curry powder
2 teaspoons cumin
1/4 teaspoon cayenne pepper
2 (15-oz) cans garbanzo beans, rinsed and drained
4 green onions, chopped
1/3 cup fresh cilantro, chopped
3 cups hot cooked couscous
6 tablespoon raisins
6 tablespoons prepared mango chutney
6 tablespoons plain yogurt

Directions:
1. Prepare the Crock-Pot with nonstick spray.

2. Place the potatoes in the bottom of the Crock-Pot.

3. In a bowl, combine the onion, garlic, carrot, tomato, bell pepper, salt, curry, cumin and cayenne and stir well. Pour over the potatoes in the Crock-Pot.

4. Add the garbanzo beans, cover and cook on low for 9 hours.

5. Stir in the green onion and cilantro and cook 10 more minutes.

6. Put some couscous in a bowl and ladle the mixture in the Crock-Pot over top. Add sweetness by adding 1 tablespoon each raisins, mango chutney and yogurt on top.

Layered Vegetable Lasagna

Layer everything into the Crock-Pot and let it go until dinnertime. How easy is that? Instead of using noodles, you use thinly sliced potatoes. I use russet, but I have also used unpeeled red potatoes and kind of like it better. The red potatoes hold up a little better. This is all made of vegetables and it is a lovely dish to serve to guests, even those that like meat.

Ingredients:
1 (14.5-oz) can of tomato sauce
1 tablespoon Italian Herbs
1/2 teaspoon salt
1/4 teaspoon pepper
4 potatoes, peeled and sliced thin
2 large zucchini, peeled and sliced thin
2 carrots, peeled and sliced thin
1/2 cup frozen corn, divided
1/2 cup frozen peas, divided
More salt and pepper to taste
1-1/2 cups shredded Cheddar

Directions:
1. Use a liner in the Crock-Pot to prevent sticking.

2. In a large bowl, combine the sauce, herbs, salt and pepper. Mix and set aside.

3. Spray the liner with nonstick spray and layer half of the potatoes on the bottom of the Crock-Pot. Cover completely and sprinkle with a pinch more of salt and pepper.

4. Layer only half of the zucchini over top the potatoes.

5. Layer in half the carrots and then half the frozen corn and peas.

6. Pour in half the sauce and sprinkle with half the cheese.

7. Put in another layer of potatoes, zucchini, carrots, corn and peas.

8. Pour in the rest of the sauce and sprinkle with the rest of the cheese.

9. Cook on high for 3 to 4 hours and serve.

Lentils and Squash over Rice
Use either red or brown lentils in this recipe and butternut squash is my preferred type. The coconut milk and tomatoes combine to make a very rich and satisfying sauce. Serve over cooked brown rice or some egg noodles for a luscious feast that is full of protein and flavor.

Ingredients:
4 cups water
1 yellow onion, peeled and diced
1 clove garlic, peeled and minced
1 large carrot, peeled and diced
2 cups red or brown lentils
2 cups butternut squash, peeled and diced
1 (14-oz) can coconut milk
1 (15-oz) can diced tomatoes with juice
1 tablespoon curry powder
1 teaspoon salt
Cooked rice

Directions:
1. Place a liner in the slow cooker and pour the water in.

2. Add the onion, garlic, carrot, lentils, squash, coconut milk, tomatoes with the juice, curry powder and salt and stir.

3. Cook 6 to 8 hours on low.

4. Serve over rice.

Spinach and Bean Enchiladas

I love enchiladas and especially the ones made with beans and no meat. This recipe has a delightful flavor using black beans, but I have substituted pinto beans and liked it just as much. This recipe will make 6 enchiladas, so if you are making it for a party, definitely double the recipe.

Ingredients:
1 (14.5-oz) can of black beans, rinsed and drained, divided
1 (10-oz) package of frozen chopped spinach, thawed
1 cup frozen corn, thawed
1/2 teaspoon cumin
1/4 teaspoon salt
1/4 teaspoon pepper
2 cups shredded sharp Cheddar cheese, divided
3 – 1/2 cups commercial or homemade salsa (2 jars commercial salsa), divided
8 – 6 inch corn tortillas, warmed
Sour cream
Green Onions, sliced thin

Directions:
1. Place half of the beans in a large bowl and mash with a fork. Add the corn. Squeeze all the liquid left in the spinach making it as dry as possible and add it to the bowl with the cumin, salt, pepper and half of the Cheddar.

2. Leave the rest of the beans whole and add to the bowl. Mix well.

3. Put a liner in a Crock-Pot and spray with nonstick spray. This will stick if you don't.

4. Spread half of the commercial salsa on the bottom of the Crock-Pot.

5. Warm the tortillas to make them pliable so they won't break.

6. Fill the tortillas with the bean mixture (about ½ cup each) and roll carefully. Place in the Crock-Pot with the seam side down.

7. Top with the rest of the salsa and cheese.

8. Cook on high for 3 hours – no longer.

9. Serve putting a dollop of sour cream on each enchilada that is sprinkled with green onion.

Stroganoff a la Mushroom
I really like this mushroom stroganoff better than the beef variety. Use any kind of mushroom you like, but since portabellas are "meatier" than other mushrooms. I use them. I get the "baby-bellas" and they seem to be tasty and fill out this recipe well. Avoid using canned mushrooms or your dish will come out slimy (yes, I did make that mistake once).

Ingredients:
2 cloves garlic, peeled and minced
1 large onion, peeled and thinly sliced
5 cups prepared mushrooms
1 – 1/2 cup vegetable stock
3 teaspoons paprika
1/2 teaspoon salt
1/4 teaspoon pepper
1/2 cup sour cream
1/4 cup fresh chopped parsley

Directions:
1. Prepare the Crock-Pot with nonstick spray.

2. Place the garlic, onions and mushrooms in the bottom of the Crock-Pot.

3. Add the vegetable stock, paprika, salt and pepper and stir to mix.

4. Cook on high for 4 hours.

5. Stir in the sour cream and cook on high, covered, for 15 more minutes.

6. Serve over cooked egg noodles and sprinkle with parsley.

Sweet Potato Vegetarian Chili
This dish is a little unusual, but you should try it for something different, especially if you like sweet potatoes. The unusual part comes from the cocoa powder and cinnamon, but it has a very pleasant flavor that you just don't want to miss.

Ingredients:
1 red onion, peeled and chopped
4 cloves garlic, peeled and chopped
1 green bell pepper, chopped
1 tablespoon chili powder
1 tablespoon cumin
2 teaspoons unsweetened cocoa powder
1/4 teaspoon ground cinnamon
1 teaspoon kosher salt
1/2 teaspoon ground black pepper
1 (15-oz) can of light kidney beans, rinsed and drained
1 (15-oz) can of black beans that have been rinsed and drained
1 (28-oz) can of diced tomatoes
1 large sweet potato, peeled and diced
1 cup water
Sour Cream
Green Onions
Tortilla Chips

Directions:
1. Prepare a Crock-Pot with nonstick spray.

2. Layer in the onion, garlic, bell pepper, chili powder, cumin, cocoa powder, cinnamon, salt and pepper and mix lightly.

3. Add the rinsed and drained kidney and black beans. Add the tomatoes with the juice.

4. Put in the sweet potato and water and cook on low 7 hours or on high 4 to 5 hours. Check to make sure the potato is tender.

5. Put in a bowl and serve with sour cream, green onion and sprinkle on tortilla chips.

Vegetable Stuffed Peppers

You simply will not miss the meat in this stuffed pepper recipe. I like to use a combination of red, yellow, orange and green peppers to make this dish very colorful.

Ingredients:
2 cups cooked and cooled brown rice
1 small sweet onion, peeled and chopped
3 small tomatoes, chopped
1 cup frozen corn kernels, thawed and drained
1/3 cup black beans, rinsed and drained
1/3 cup kidney beans, rinsed and drained
3/4 cup Monterey Jack cheese, cubed
4 fresh basil leaves, thinly sliced
3 cloves garlic, minced
1/2 teaspoon salt
1/4 teaspoon pepper
3/4 cup meatless spaghetti sauce
½ cup water
6 large bell peppers, hollowed
4 tablespoons Parmesan cheese, divided

Directions:
1. Prior to starting, the night before or morning, cook the brown rice and let it cool.

2. In a bowl, combine the onion, tomatoes, thawed corn, both beans, cheese cubes, basil, garlic, salt and pepper and mix gently to combine.

3. In another bowl combine the sauce and water and whisk together.

4. Prepare a Crock-Pot with a liner.

5. Pour half of the sauce mixture in the bottom of the Crock-Pot.

6. Fill the 6 peppers with the vegetable mixture and set them in the Crock-Pot.

7. Pour the rest of the sauce over top and sprinkle with just 2 tablespoons of the Parmesan.

8. Cook on low 3 to 4 hours or until the peppers are tender. Sprinkle with the other 2 tablespoons of Parmesan and serve.

Vegetarian Sloppy Joes
Instead of ground beef, this recipe uses pinto beans. Make it spicy by using black beans or use Great Northern beans for a different flavor. It will be good anyway you make it.

Ingredients:
1 -1/2 tablespoon olive oil
2 cloves garlic, peeled and minced
1 large white onion, peeled and sliced thin
2 medium carrots, peeled and sliced thin
2 tablespoons Balsamic vinegar
2 tablespoons chili powder
1 large red bell pepper, seeded and chopped
1 cup dry pinto beans, rinsed and drained
1/2 cup water
1 (8-oz) can tomato sauce
2 tablespoons tomato paste
2 tablespoons soy sauce
4 cups cabbage, thinly sliced
1 zucchini, chopped
1 cup frozen corn kernels, thawed
2 tablespoons honey mustard
1 teaspoon salt
1 tablespoon brown sugar
8 to 10 hamburger buns (whole wheat preferred)

Directions:
1. Heat a skillet over medium heat and add the olive oil. Put in the garlic, onion and carrots and sauté for about 6

minutes. Remove from the heat and put in the vinegar and chili powder. Stir well and set aside.

2. Prepare the Crock-Pot with nonstick spray and pour in the rinsed and drained beans. Add the bell pepper, water, tomato sauce, tomato paste, and soy. Stir well.

3. Spread the garlic, onion, carrot mixture on top. This will weight down the beans so they will be immersed in liquid and stay tender.

4. Cook on low 5 hours or on high 9 hours.

5. Add the cabbage, zucchini and corn. Stir in the mustard, salt and brown sugar and continue to cook on high 30 more minutes.

6. Serve on buns.

Chapter 8: World Class Breakfast and Lunch Recipes

I love putting on the Crock-Pot when I go to bed at night and when I get up breakfast is ready. Make eggs, oatmeal and even a delicious French Toast. The Crock-Pot is a good tool for making sandwich fillings too. The Philly beef recipe is good, but so is everything else.

Apple Cinnamon Oatmeal in a Crock-Pot

This sweet and delicious oatmeal cooks in 7 hours, so if that is how long you are going to sleep, you can put it on before bed and get up with breakfast ready. It is going to be one of your family's favorite breakfast items.

Ingredients:
1-1/2 cups water
1-1/2 cups coconut milk
2 tablespoons brown sugar
1 tablespoon coconut oil
2 peeled, cored and diced apples
1 teaspoon cinnamon
1/4 teaspoon salt
1 cup Steel Cut oats
Chopped nuts as garnish

Directions:
1. Prepare a Crock-Pot with nonstick spray.

2. Put all ingredients except the chopped nuts in the Crock-Pot and stir to combine well.

3. Cook on low 5 to 7 hours or on high 3 hours.

4. Top with nuts before you serve.

Biscuits and Gravy

This old fashioned recipe comes from the South and from a long time ago. It has been modernized by cooking it in a slow cooker, but it tastes just as good. This recipe has fennel seed added to it and it makes the flavor a little brighter. Try it with the fennel, and if you don't like the flavor, omit it the next time. The fennel does help to break down the heaviness of the gravy. Get the ready-made biscuits in a can to make this go a little easier.

Ingredients:
1 pound bulk pork sausage
2 tablespoons butter
2 tablespoons flour
1 cup milk
1 (10.5-oz) can cream of mushroom soup
½ teaspoon fennel seed, crushed
4 (6-oz) cans of large buttermilk biscuits

Directions:
1. Heat a skillet and add the sausage. Brown for 5 to 7 minutes until there is no pink visible. Use a slotted spoon to put into a large bowl.

2. Use the same skillet and place the butter in to melt. Add the flour and whisk until there are no lumps. Add the milk slowly, whisking constantly until it starts to thicken, about 2 to 3 minutes.

3. Remove the skillet from the heat and stir in the soup and fennel seed with the whisk.

4. Prepare a slow cooker with nonstick spray.

5. Separate the biscuits into 10 sections and cut in quarter. Roll and place on the bottom and sides of the slow cooker.

6. Pour the sauce slowly into the biscuits in the slow cooker.

7. Place a triple layer of white paper towels over top of everything in the Crock-Pot and put the lid on. This will keep the recipe from drying out.

8. Cook low 3-1/2 to 4-1/2 hours or until the biscuits turn golden brown.

9. Serve by scooping out some and putting it in a bowl.

Crock-Pot Eggs and Sausage

This is a great recipe for a Saturday or Sunday brunch when you don't have to be anywhere in 3 hours. Do not cook overnight because it will be completely overdone. It only takes 3 hours to cook, so you can get up at a decent hour on the weekend, put it on and have brunch at 10 or 11 am.

Ingredients:

1 20-oz) bag of frozen hash browns, thawed and drained
1 pound bulk sausage
12 eggs
3/4 cup half and half
1/2 teaspoon red pepper flakes, crushed
1/2 teaspoon salt
1/4 teaspoon pepper
1/2 cup green onion, chopped
1/2 cup red pepper. Seeded and chopped
2 cups shredded Cheddar (you can use Monterey Jack or Swiss to switch it up)

Directions:

1. Make sure the hash browns are drained and dried by squeezing between paper towels. Get as much moisture out as possible and set aside.

2. In a skillet, brown the sausage and set aside.

3. In a bowl, whisk the eggs and half and half. Add red pepper flakes, salt and pepper and whisk well.

4. Place the chopped onions in one bowl and the chopped red pepper in another bowl. Set aside.

5. Prepare a Crock-Pot with a liner and spray the liner with nonstick spray.

6. Put half of the hash browns in the bottom and layer on half the sausage, half the green onions and half the red peppers. Put a layer of cheese on top.

7. Do another layer of hash browns, sausage, green onion and pepper and sprinkle on half of the cheese you have left reserving the rest for later.

8. Slowly and carefully pour the egg mixture over top and try not to dislodge the layers.

9. Cook on low 4 to 5 hours and high 2-1/2 to 3 hours. Check for doneness by inserting a meat thermometer. This is the safest way to make sure it is done and no one will get sick. The thermometer should read 160 degrees F.

10. Sprinkle the rest of the cheese over before serving.

Cuban Flank Sandwich with Kick

This is a twist on a Cuban sandwich and it is very spicy with lots of cumin, garlic powder, pepper flakes and such. The recipe calls for commercial picadillo sauce and I like it that way. If you can't find picadillo, just use pickle relish instead.

Ingredients:
2 large onion, peeled and cut into thin slices
½ teaspoon salt
1-1/4 teaspoon pepper
1-1/4 teaspoon garlic powder
1-1/4 teaspoon onion powder
1-1/4 teaspoon cumin
1-1/4 teaspoon dried oregano
1 teaspoon red pepper flakes, crushed
1 – 2-pound beef flank
1-1/4 cup beef broth
1/3 cup lime juice
Cuban or Kaiser rolls
Commercial picadillo or pickle relish

Directions:
1- Prepare a Crock-Pot by spraying with nonstick spray.

2- In a bowl, combine the salt, pepper, garlic powder, onion powder, cumin, oregano and pepper flakes.

3- Rub this mixture onto the beef flank top and bottom. Cut crosswise into 4 pieces and put into the Crock-Pot bottom.

4- Carefully pour the broth around the sides of the beef.

5- Cook on low for 8 to 9 hours or on high for 4 to 4-1/2 hours. Remove the meat and place on a cutting board to cool a few minutes. Shred the beef with 2 forks and return to the Crock-Pot with the lime juice. Heat through.

6- Spread the rolls with picadillo or pickle relish and use a slotted spoon to get the meat out of the Crock-Pot to the sandwich. Cover with the top of the bun and serve.

Ham, Spinach and Egg Hot Dish

When I make a ham, I always have leftovers and this is a delicious way to use it up without making another dinner or having ham sandwiches. You need a big bowl for this recipe because you mix everything in it before putting it in the Crock-Pot.

Ingredients:
6 eggs
1/2 cup Greek yogurt
1/4 cup milk
1 clove garlic, minced
1/2 medium onion, peeled and chopped
1/2 teaspoon thyme
1/2 teaspoon salt
1/4 teaspoon pepper
1/3 cup mushrooms, diced
1 cup baby spinach packed
1 cup shredded pepper jack cheese
1 cup cooked, diced ham

Directions:
1. In a very large bowl, whisk the eggs with the yogurt and milk.

2. Add the garlic, onion, thyme, salt, pepper and mix well.

3. Add mushrooms, spinach, pepper jack and the ham and mix well.

4. Prepare a Crock-Pot with a liner and spray with nonstick spray. This tends to stick.

5. Cook on high 90 minutes to 2 hours on high or until it becomes set. Slice and serve hot.

Holiday French Toast in A Crock-Pot with Chocolate Chips
My family has always served this dish on Christmas morning because you just make it the night before and someone gets up before everyone else and puts it on so it cooks in enough time to eat after presents are opened. Sometimes it is the only thing that gets the kids away from their new toys. This must be refrigerated overnight. If you don't do that, it won't turn out very well and be very sloppy.

Ingredients:
1 pound French bread, cut in 1 inch cubes
1-1/2 cup milk
3 eggs
3/4 cup packed brown sugar
1 teaspoon vanilla
1 teaspoon cinnamon
1 cup semisweet chocolate chips

Directions:
1. Put a liner in the Crock-Pot and spray it with nonstick spray.

2. Place the French bread in the bottom of the Crock-Pot.

3. In a large bowl, whisk the milk and eggs. Add the brown sugar, vanilla and cinnamon and mix well.

4. Pour the milk and egg mixture over top the bread and put the covered crock in the refrigerator overnight.

5. Sprinkle the chocolate chips on top and put the crock into the sleeve. Turn it on low and cook 4 hours. Don't try to cook on high for half the time, it will burn.

Mexican Huevos Rancheros
This egg dish can also be served on corn tortillas that have been steamed along with some avocado or sour cream, green onion, some cilantro and a squire of lime juice. It makes for a great roll up sandwich to eat on the go. The whole family will want 1 or 2.

My sister gets up to run at 5 am and she pulls this out of the refrigerator (she prepared it the night before) and puts it in the slow cooker and turns it on. It is ready after she gets back, takes a shower, gets the kids and husband up and everyone is ready to go around 7 to 7:30 am.

Ingredients:
10 eggs
1 cup half and half
12 ounces shredded Monterey Jack cheese
1 clove minced garlic
1 (4-oz) can of chopped green chili
1/2 teaspoon chili powder
1/2 teaspoon pepper
1 (10-oz) ounce bottle salsa or homemade salsa

Directions:
1. In a large bowl, break the eggs and whisk them with the half and half.

2. Whisk in half of the shredded cheese.

3. Add the garlic, green chilies, chili powder and pepper.

4. Prepare a slow cooker with nonstick spray and pour the ingredients in.

5. Cover and cook on low for 2 hours.

6. Serve on a plate by itself or with a corn tortilla. Top with salsa and sprinkle in more cheese.

Philly-Inspired Cheese Sandwich Filling
These sandwiches are not totally like a traditional Philly cheese, in fact, they might be better. The filling is very easy to make and you just must put it on a hoagie or Kaiser roll to serve.

Ingredients:
2-1/2-pound boneless beef chuck pot roast
2 cloves garlic, peeled and minced
1 cup onion, peeled and chopped
1/2 cup beef broth
1/4 cup Worcestershire sauce

1 teaspoon dried oregano
1/2 teaspoon dried thyme
1/2 teaspoon dried basil
1 cup pickled peppers, or sautéed red or green bell peppers
Slices of Provolone cheese

Directions:

1. Trim the fat from the pot roast and slice it in thin strips

2. Prepare a slow cooker with nonstick spray and place the strips in the bottom.

3. Add the garlic, onion, broth, Worcestershire sauce, oregano, thyme and basil. If you are using saluted bell peppers, put them in now. If you are using the pickled peppers, wait until later to add them.

4. Cook 10 to 12 hours on low or on high 5 to 6 hours. Stir occasionally to keep the meat from sticking.

5. If you are using pickled peppers, add them when there is 30 more minutes of cooking time.

6. Place the meat mixture on toasted hoagie or Kaiser buns and put a few slices of Provolone on top. Put under the broiler until the cheese melts and serve.

Rustic Chicken and Pepper Sandwiches
The chicken is shredded in this recipe and the combination with roasted red peppers is absolutely delightful. There is even pesto on this sandwich making it richly flavorful.

Ingredients:
1-1/4-pound boneless chicken thighs
2 cloves minced garlic
1/2 cup roasted red bell pepper (from a jar or roast yourself and chop)
1/2 teaspoon salt
1/4 cup mayonnaise
3 tablespoons pesto
Focaccia or Kaiser rolls
Sliced tomatoes

Directions:
1. Prepare a Crock-Pot with nonstick spray.

2. Place the whole chicken thighs in the bottom and sprinkle the garlic and peppers over top with the salt.

3. Cook on low 6 to 7 hours or on high 4 hours.

4. Remove the chicken thighs and place on a cutting board. Use 2 forks to shred the meat and add it back to the Crock-Pot.

5. While the chicken is reheating, mix the mayonnaise and the pesto in a small bowl.

6. Cut focaccia in wedges or open the Kaiser rolls in half. Spread the mayonnaise mixture on the top. Use a slotted spoon to pull out about 1/3 cup of the chicken and pepper filling and place it on top. Put a tomato slice on to finish off and serve.

Sweet and Savory Ham Sandwiches

If you put this on in the morning, it will be ready for lunch at noon. This sandwich is a favorite at parties too because of its sweet flavor from the apples and smoky notes from paprika.

Ingredients:
3 pounds of thin sliced deli ham
1/2 cup sweet pickle relish
2/3 cup packed brown sugar
2 teaspoons prepared brown or yellow mustard
1 teaspoon paprika
2 cups apple juice

Directions:
1. Prepare the Crock-Pot by spraying with nonstick spray.

2. Separate the deli ham slices and place them in the bottom of the Crock-Pot layering them one by one. You don't want them to stick together.

3. In a bowl, combine the pickle relish, brown sugar, mustard and paprika. Add the apple juice and mix well.

4. Pour the sugar mixture over top the ham in the Crock-Pot.

5. Cook on low 4 to 5 hours

6. Open a Kaiser roll and place 3 to 4 slices of the ham inside. Add a little more pickle relish if desired.

Taste of Summer Fair Sausage and Pepper Sandwiches
Our county fair serves these delightful sandwiches and I just don't like to wait until August to have one. I can make them in my Crock-Pot anytime I want. Use sweet, hot or mild sausage in bulk and green, red, or yellow bell peppers.

Ingredients:
1 teaspoon olive oil
2 cloves garlic, peeled and minced
1 large sweet onion, peeled and thin sliced
20 ounces of Italian sausage
1 large green bell pepper, seeded and sliced in strips
2 large red bell peppers, seeded and sliced in strips
1 large yellow bell pepper, seeded and sliced in strips
1/4 cup red wine vinegar
1/2 teaspoon pepper
1/2 teaspoon thyme
2 tablespoons water
1-1/2 tablespoon cornstarch
1 teaspoon prepared brown mustard
Hoagie rolls
Slices of Provolone cheese

Directions:
1. Put a skillet on the stove over medium high heat and pour in the olive oil.

2. Sauté the garlic and onion for about 3 minutes and add the sausage. Stir constantly to brown the sausage. Remove with a slotted spoon and drain on paper towels.

3. Prepare a Crock-Pot with nonstick spray.

4. Place the meat mixture in the bottom and add the bell peppers, vinegar, pepper and thyme.

5. Cook on high 3 hours or on low 6 hours. Low is better because the flavors mingle more.

6. Remove all the solids from the Crock-Pot with a slotted spoon and place in a bowl. Pour the left-over liquid into a sauce pan.

7. In a small bowl, combine the water and cornstarch and whisk well. Add to the saucepan along with the mustard and bring to a boil. Boil for 1 minute stirring constantly. The mixture should thicken.

8. Toast the hoagie buns on a broiler and fill them with the meat mixture. Drizzle a little juice in the saucepan over top and put a slice of Provolone on before putting the top on. Serve while hot.

The Best Roast Beef Sandwich Filling
Forget about going out to get a good roast beef sandwich. You can make it right at home in your own Crock-Pot and serve with melted Provolone in a Kaiser roll.

Ingredients:
1 – 3 to 4 pound beef rump roast
1 envelope onion soup mix
2 ribs celery that have been chopped fine
1 (14.5-oz) can cream of mushroom soup
1 (6-oz) jar of sliced mushrooms that have been drained well

Directions:
1. Prepare the Crock-Pot with nonstick spray.

2. Cut the roast to fit inside the bottom of the Crock-Pot, if necessary.

3. In a bowl, combine the soup mix, celery and the cream of mushroom soup. Pour this mixture over the roast in the Crock-Pot.

4. Cook for 8 to 10 hours on low. This tenderizes the roast, so do not cook on high.

5. An hour before you plan to serve, remove the roast from the Crock-Pot and let it sit 10 minutes on a cutting board. Take 2 forks and shred the meat.

6. Put the shredded beef back in the Crock-Pot and add the drained mushrooms.

7. Cook just until heated through and put about ½ cup on each Kaiser roll.

Chapter 9: Deserts and Other Treats Slow Cooked to Sweet Tasty Perfection

A friend of mine had a college student in culinary school and in the dorm, they made cakes in their Crock-Pot. I was down for that, but there is more than just cakes to be made this way. Try apple crisp or rice pudding too. They were almost better than making it in an oven. Put a liner in a Crock-Pot and make candy for a no fuss, easy clean experience.

Chocoholic Chocolate Cake in a Crock-Pot
This cake is super chocolate delicious because it uses chocolate pudding, chocolate chips and chocolate cake mix. My mom was a true chocoholic. We had to hide the Halloween candy every year and hope she didn't sniff it out. She would start at one end of the Crock-Pot and eat her way all the way through to the other side with this cake and it doesn't have frosting.

Ingredients
1 regular sized chocolate cake mix
1 (3.9-oz) package of instant chocolate pudding mix
1 cup water
3/4 cup vegetable oil
4 large eggs, slightly beaten
1 (16-oz) container of sour cream
1 (6-oz) package of semisweet chocolate chips

Directions:
1. Empty the cake and pudding mix into a large bowl and whisk it to combine well.

2. In a mixer bowl, add the water and vegetable oil. Beat while dropping in the eggs and beat until frothy.

3. Beat in the sour cream.

4. Stir in the chocolate chips by hand.

5. Prepare a 5-quart Crock-Pot with nonstick spray and pour the batter in.

6. Cook on low 6 to 8 hours. Insert a knife in the center and if nothing much sticks, it is done.

7. Serve warm in bowls with whipped cream on top.

Chocolate Fudge in a Crock-Pot

This fudge is very creamy and delicious. The coconut milk and coconut sugar are used because it is less likely to burn than regular milk and sugar having a higher burn point. This recipe uses semi-sweet chocolate chips, but you can substitute milk chocolate if you like that better. I have also used peppermint or almond flavoring rather than vanilla.

Ingredients:

2-1/2 cups semi-sweet chocolate chips
1/2 cup canned coconut milk
1 dash of sea salt
1/4 cup coconut sugar
2 tablespoons coconut oil
1-1/2 teaspoon vanilla

Directions:

1. Prepare a Crock-Pot with nonstick spray. I have used a liner with better results.

2. Pour the chocolate chips in the bottom of the Crock-Pot.

3. In a large bowl, combine the coconut milk, salt, coconut sugar and coconut oil

4. Cook on low 2 hours and do not lift the lid.

5. Turn the Crock-Pot off and remove the lid to add the vanilla or other flavoring. Check the mixture with a candy thermometer to make sure it is 110 degrees F or cooler.

6. With a wooden spoon, stir vigorously for 5 to 8 minutes or until the fudge loses its glossy appearance and becomes dull.

7. Put vegetable oil on an 8 by 8-inch square pan and pour the hot fudge in. Cover with plastic wrap and refrigerate at least 4 hours or overnight.

8. Cut into squares and keep in an airtight container in the refrigerator.

Creamy and Delicious Rice Pudding

Rice pudding is just one of those things no one makes much anymore, but it used to be a very popular sweet treat back in the day. I love rice pudding and making it in a Crock-Pot makes it much easier. We always had rice pudding at Christmas, but with this recipe, you can have it anytime.

Ingredients:
2 lightly beaten eggs
1/2 cup uncooked rice (Use converted rice)
1/2 cup sugar
1/2 cup raisins
1-1/4 cups milk
1 teaspoon melted butter
1 teaspoon cinnamon
1-1/2 teaspoon vanilla
1/2 teaspoon lemon extract (optional – it gives some brightness to the dish)
1 cup heavy whipping cream that has been whipped up (make a little more for garnish)

Directions:
1. Prepare a Crock-Pot with nonstick spray

2. In a small bowl, beat the eggs.

3. In a separate bowl, combine the rice, sugar, raisins, cinnamon, vanilla and lemon extract. Mix together and add the beaten eggs.

4. Pour into the Crock-Pot and cook low 2 hours. Stir and cook another hour or until the rice becomes tender.

5. Transfer all the pudding to a bowl and cook 1 hour. Cover with plastic wrap and put in the refrigerator until chilled.

6. Whip the heavy cream right before serving and serve on top with a little shake of pure cinnamon.

Crock-Pot Bananas Foster (Yes, really)
Use dark rum in the Crock-Pot to make bananas foster. The alcohol will not burn off, so avoid this recipe if you do have a problem with alcohol. You can get away with adding ½ cup coconut milk instead of ¼ cup and using 2 teaspoons of rum flavor, but it won't be the same. This makes 2 large servings, so double it for more.

Ingredients:
3 tablespoons butter, cut in chunks
½ cup dark brown sugar, packed
¼ cup light unsweetened coconut milk
¼ cup dark rum
4 ripe bananas cut in ½ inch slices
1 cup fresh pineapple cut in 1 inch cubes
¼ teaspoon cinnamon
Vanilla ice cream

Directions:
1. Prepare the Crock-Pot by spraying with nonstick spray.

2. In the bottom layer the butter, brown sugar, coconut milk, and rum.

3. Cook on low 1 hour and whisk until smooth.

4. Add the bananas, pineapple and cinnamon and stir to coat with the sauce.

5. Cover and cook 15 more minutes.

6. Serve with ice cream.

Crock-Pot Dump Cherry Dessert
Make this with cherry pie filling or substitute with peach, blueberry or apple to make it different. I would use a little nutmeg and cinnamon with peach and apple instead of just cinnamon. Taking the lid off the Crock-Pot the last 30 minutes makes the consistency a little crunchy and delicious. I would say it is more like pie than cake.

Ingredients:

2 (21-oz) cans cherry pie filling
1 box of yellow cake mix
1 cup butter, melted

Directions:

1. Prepare a Crock-Pot with nonstick spray.

2. Pour both cans of pie filling in the bottom of the Crock-Pot.

3. Dump the cake mix over top.

4. Drizzle the butter over top and do not stir.

5. Cook on high about 3 hours on high.

6. Remove the cover and cook 30 more minutes and serve. I love it with ice cream.

Crock-Pot Nut Clusters

This recipe uses a variety of nuts, but you can use just one kind if you like. It makes a lot of candy. I have even reduced some of the nuts and put in dried fruit like apricot or pineapple bits. Mango bits are also pretty good. You can also use all milk chocolate if you desire.

Ingredients:
3-1/2 cups roasted and salted peanuts
3-1/2 cups toasted pecans
3-1/2 cups toasted walnuts
1 (12-oz) package of milk chocolate
1 (12-oz) package of semi-sweet chocolate
1/4 cup powdered bittersweet chocolate or 2 ounces of solid bittersweet chocolate

Directions:

1. Prepare a Crock-Pot with nonstick spray.

2. Layer in all the nights and the chocolate as they come in the recipe ingredients.

3. Cook on low 1 hour or until melted.

4. Stir and cook 2 minutes more uncovered and stir again.

5. Scoop out spoonful and place them on wax paper to cool and harden completely.

6. Once totally cool, store in an airtight container.

Easy Caramel Toffee Candy in a Crock-Pot

I love caramel and this recipe is so easy, you will want to make it over and over. Store finished product in airtight containers if you have the will-power to leave them alone until they cool and harden.

Ingredients:
1 bag caramel squares, unwrapped
12 ounces of semi-sweet chocolate chips
1 – 8 oz bag of Heath ToffeeBits

Directions:
1. Use a liner to line the Crock-Pot and spray with nonstick spray.

2. Dump in the caramels, chocolate chips and Toffeebits.

3. Cook low for 2 hours (it is done when everything melts and might take less than 2 hours).

4. Mix everything well and scoop out by teaspoonful onto wax paper covering a baking sheet.

5. Let cool and harden.

Mocha Center Chocolate Cake

This cake is meant to be served warm because the middle is like molten chocolate and it should flow out when cut into. Use an electric mixer to mix the batter or use an old fashioned hand mixer. It needs more than just a spoon can do. Use a smaller Crock-Pot too because the batter is too thin in a large and will burn. Serve with whipped cream and strawberries or raspberries on top with a sprinkle of powder sugar since there is no frosting. It is also good with ice cream.

Ingredients:

4 large eggs
1-1/2 cup granulated sugar
1/2 cup melted butter
3 teaspoons vanilla
1/2 cup powdered cocoa
1 cup flour
1/4 teaspoon salt
1 tablespoon instant coffee

Directions:
1. In a large bowl, beat the eggs and add the sugar, butter and vanilla. Mix to combine.

2. In a separate bowl, combine the cocoa, flower, salt and instant coffee and whisk to combine.

3. Gradually add the cocoa mixture to the egg mixture beating in after every addition.

4. Prepare a 1-1/2-quart Crock-Pot with nonstick spray.
5. Cook on low 3 hours. When it is done a knife or toothpick should come out with moist crumbs and cake should be somewhat firm.

6. Scoop out with a spoon to a bowl.

Moist and Luscious Sour Cream Cheese Cake
I love cheese cakes and this one is one of my favorites. It isn't dense like a regular New York cheese cake, but it does have that sour cream flavor. I use almond extract in mine because I like the taste of almond. If you don't, use vanilla instead. This recipe utilizes a spring form pan that is placed in the Crock-Pot on top of a rack. Don't try doing it without these things or it will not turn out right. I use an 8" spring form pan because it fits in my Crock-Pot.

Ingredients:
3/4 cup fine graham cracker crumbs
1/4 teaspoon cinnamon
1 pinch salt
1 tablespoon granulated sugar

2-1/2 tablespoons unsalted butter, melted
1/4 teaspoon salt
2/3 cup more granulated sugar
2 large eggs
1 teaspoon almond extract
1 cup sour cream

Directions:

1. In a bowl, combine the graham cracker crumbs, cinnamon, pinch of salt and sugar and whisk together to incorporate. Add the melted butter and stir with a fork making sure everything is coated.

2. Prepare a spring form pan with nonstick spray and place the graham cracker mixture in pressing it to the bottom and up the sides about 1 inch.

3. In a mixing bowl combine the ¼ teaspoon salt, 2/3 cup sugar and eggs. Mix until smooth and add the almond extract and sour cream. Beat until creamy.

4. Pour into the spring form pan.

5. Fill the Crock-Pot with ½ inch water and place the rack in the bottom. Put the spring form pan inside on the rack.

6. Place a triple layer of paper towels over the opening of the Crock-Pot and put the lid on to secure them so they don't fall into the cheese cake.

7. Cook high 2 hours.

8. Turn the Crock-Pot off and let stand for 1 hour. Do not lift the lid.

9. The spring form will be warm but you should be able to lift it out with some long tongs. Place it on a cooling rack for 1 hour and wrap with plastic wrap and put in the refrigerator at least 4 hours to overnight.

10. Run a knife around the edges of the pan before releasing and sliding them off. Cut in wedges and serve.

Old-fashioned Apple Crisp in a Crock-Pot

My grandmother made apple crisp and I always thought it was the best, especially when served with a scoop of vanilla ice cream. Make a modernized Crock-Pot version with biscuit mix. That cinnamon sweetness mingles with the apples to make a sweet treat. Cooking apples do best in a Crock-Pot because they are firm and don't become mushy. I use Macintosh apples because they work the best for me.

Ingredients:
1/2 teaspoon ground cinnamon
1/2 cup granulated sugar
6 cups cooking apples, cored and sliced
1 cup biscuit mix
1/2 cup quick cooking oatmeal
1/3 cup packed brown sugar
1/4 cup granulated sugar
1/4 teaspoon salt
1/4 teaspoon cinnamon
1/4 teaspoon nutmeg
1/2 cup cold butter that has been cut into small pieces

Directions:
1. In a medium bowl, mix the sugar and cinnamon until well combined.

2. Place the prepared apples in the bowl and make sure all of the slices are coated with the mixture.

3. Prepare a Crock-Pot with nonstick spray and arrange the apple mixture in the bottom.

4. In a separate bowl, combine the biscuit mix, oatmeal, both sugars, salt, cinnamon, and nutmeg. Combine with a whisk and incorporate the butter with a fork or pastry cutter until the mixture is crumbly.

5. Sprinkle over the apples and cook on high for 3 hours. Watch that it doesn't burn.

6. Serve with ice cream.

Peanut Butter Fudge

This recipe makes a creamy and decadent peanut butter fudge that is beyond compare. When it cools, slice it in squares and store in an airtight container. Use a 4 to 5-quart Crock-Pot to make this fudge.

Ingredients:

3 cups semi-sweet chocolate chips
1 tablespoon salted butter
¾ cup smooth peanut butter
1-(14-oz) can sweetened, condensed milk
1 teaspoon vanilla

Directions:

1. Prepare the Crock-Pot with nonstick spray.

2. Layer in the chocolate chips, butter, peanut butter, condensed milk and stir.

3. Cook on low for 2 hours, stirring occasionally.

4. Line a 9 by 9-inch baking pan with parchment paper.

5. Pour in the fudge from the Crock-Pot and let set 4 hours.

6. Cut in squares.

Pineapple Upside Down Cake A La Crock-Pot

When you are done baking this cake, you must remove the crock and turn it upside down on a cutting board, so make sure you can do this. It is best to make it in a 6-quart Crock-Pot and you cannot use a liner. You must coat the inside with a lot of nonstick spray.

Ingredients:

1/4 cup melted butter
1 cup packed brown sugar
1 (20-oz) can pineapple slices in juice
10 – Maraschino cherries drained with stems removed
1 cup combination of juice from the pineapple and water
1 regular box yellow super moist cake mix
Vegetable oil as called for with the cake mix
Eggs as called for with the cake mix

Directions:

1. Prepare the Crock-Pot with nonstick spray on the bottom and up the sides. Don't miss any spots.

2. In a bowl, combine the melted butter and brown sugar and distribute it evenly on the bottom of the crock.

3. Drain the juice from the pineapple into a measuring cup and set aside. Place the pineapple slices over the butter and sugar mixture. Try to cover the entire bottom by cutting the slices so they fit right to the edge.

4. Place cherries in the holes where the core was.

5. Add enough water to the pineapple juice in the measuring cup to make 1 cup and set aside.

6. Mix the cake mix per package instructions and pour over the pineapple slices.

7. Cook high 2-1/2 to 3 hours or until a knife comes out clean when pressed into the center of the cake.

8. Turn off the Crock-Pot and remove the ceramic bowl placing it on a rack to cook 15 minutes.

9. Put a heatproof platter or cutting board over the opening of the Crock-Pot and quickly turn it upside down. The cake should fall out. Serve warm.

Slow Cooker Bread Pudding

I always end up with bread that gets a little tough and stale, but is not moldy yet. I use it up by making bread pudding. This particular recipe is cinnamon bread pudding but you can also add about ¼ cup chocolate chips on top to make it chocolaty too. Use a liner for this recipe or you might have to get the residue off with dynamite.

Ingredients:

8 cups stale white bread or day-old French bread cut in 1 inch cubes
1/2 cup golden raisins
4 eggs
1/4 cup melted butter

2 cups milk
1 cup granulated sugar
1/4 teaspoon nutmeg
1 teaspoon cinnamon
1/8 teaspoon salt
1/2 teaspoon vanilla extract

Directions:

1. Place a liner in the Crock-Pot and spray with nonstick spray.

2. Cut the bread cubes and arrange at the bottom of the Crock-Pot and sprinkle the raisins over top.

3. In a bowl, beat the eggs and add the melted butter and milk. Whisk well.

4. In a small bowl, combine the sugar, cinnamon, nutmeg and salt. Whisk the sugar mixture into the egg mixture and add the vanilla.

5. Pour the egg mixture over the bread in the Crock-Pot and cook on low 3 hours. Check with a toothpick to make sure it comes out clean.

6. Serve warm with whipped cream or ice cream.

Sweet and Spicy Apple Sauce

My mom used to make homemade applesauce and it is absolutely the best when it is still warm. Cooking this in the Crock-Pot makes it so it is warm when you eat it. I like to make my apple sauce chunky, but if you like it smoother, just use an immersion blender to get all the lumps out.

Ingredients

8 to 10 cooking apples, peeled, cored and sliced thin
1-1/2 teaspoons ground cinnamon
1/2 cup granulated sugar
1/2 cup water

Directions:

1. Prepare a Crock-Pot with nonstick spray.

2. Place the apples in the bottom.

3. In a bowl, mix the cinnamon with the sugar and sprinkle over top of the apple slices. Use a spoon to make sure that all the slices are coated.

4. Pour the water around the edges of the Crock-Pot.

5. Cook low 6 to 8 hours. The apples should be soft. Stir every once in a while to make sure the sugar does not burn on the Crock-Pot and the apples break down.

6. Use an immersion blender to smooth the sauce, if desired.

Chapter 10: Sweet and Spicy Sauces and Condiments

Spaghetti and Alfredo sauce is super easy to make in a Crock-Pot, but did you know you can make salsa and ketchup too. Many of these sauces are easy to freeze for future use, so get several Crock-Pots going on a Saturday and make a bunch of sauce to be used throughout the week. Make your own condiments too.

Creamy Alfredo Sauce
Some people don't like Alfredo sauce because they feel it is bland. Not This Alfredo Sauce. It is delightfully flavored with garlic, butter and Parmesan and makes for a luscious dinner. I do not try to freeze this sauce as it sometimes will separate. You really don't have to worry much about leftovers though. It will be gone when dinner is done. You can serve on top of pasta with a hot cooked chicken breast sliced on top.

Ingredients:
2 cups heavy whipping cream
3-1/3 cups chicken broth
4 cloves of garlic, peeled and minced
1/2 cup soft butter
1/2 cup flour
1/4 cup fresh parsley that has been finely chopped
1 cup Parmesan cheese grated from the block

Directions:
1. Use a liner for your slow cooker for this recipe.

2. In a bowl, whisk the cream and broth until well incorporated and stir in the garlic. Pour into the slow cooker.

3. Cook on low 4 to 5 hours.

4. About 30 minutes before it is done, take bowl and whisk the butter, flour and parsley until smooth. Scrape it into the slow cooker and stir until completely melted. Cook for 30 minutes more. The sauce should thicken.

5. When done, stir in the grated Parmesan and serve.

Crock-Pot Coney Sauce

Coney sauce comes from the past and summertime at the beach. It is a chunky sauce with ground beef in it that is tangy from vinegar and spices and sweet from ketchup. This sauce freezes well and only takes a little while to defrost. Serve it with hotdogs at parties or backyard barbeques. You can make it mild or spicy purely by adjusting the amount of hot sauce you put in. The 2 drops in the recipe are for mild sauce, but I have known people to put in as much as 5 drops for a spicy sauce.

Ingredients:

1 teaspoon olive oil
1 clove garlic, peeled and minced
1 small onion, peeled and chopped
2 pounds ground beef
2 drops hot sauce
3/4 teaspoon Worcestershire sauce
1-1/2 cups ketchup
1/4 cup granulated sugar
1/4 cup white vinegar
1/4 cup prepared yellow mustard
1/4 teaspoon salt
1/4 teaspoon pepper
1/2 teaspoon celery seed

Directions:

1. In a skillet over medium heat, pour the olive oil and sauté the garlic and onion about 4 minutes.

2. Add ground beef and brown completely. Drain grease

3. Prepare a Crock-Pot with nonstick spray and pour in the ingredients in the skillet.

4. Place the rest of the ingredients in the Crock-Pot and stir well.

5. Cook on low for 3 hours and serve right from the Crock-Pot.

Fancy Beef and Red Wine Sauce

This recipe makes a gourmet meal that is absolutely delicious. If you do not want to use the wine, you can substitute ½ cup more beef broth and ½ cup water, but it isn't going to taste as good. It will just be a plain beef sauce. I freeze this for when unexpected company comes and it keeps nicely in the freezer.

Ingredients:
1 tablespoon olive oil
1 medium onion, peeled and sliced thin
1 clove garlic, peeled and minced
3 pounds boneless beef chuck roast cut into 1 inch pieces
1 pound fresh whole mushrooms cut in half
1 (1.61-oz) package brown gravy mix
1 cup red wine
1 (10.5-oz) can beef broth
2 tablespoons tomato paste
1 bay leaf

Directions:
1. Put a skillet on the stove over medium high heat and add olive oil.

2. Sauté the garlic and onion for 4 minutes.

3. Add the beef and brown it on all sides.

4. Add the mushrooms and sauté 3 more minutes.

5. Prepare a Crock-Pot with nonstick spray and pour the ingredients in the skillet in.

6. Sprinkle gravy mix over top and pour in the wine and beef broth.

7. Add tomato paste and stir well. Add the bay leaf.

8. Cook on high for 6 hours.

9. Remove the bay leaf and serve over egg noodles.

Homemade Ketchup Made in a Crock-Pot

If you make this ketchup you may never go back to store-bought brands again. It is so flavorful and delicious and easy to make. Once you make it and bottle it, it must be kept in the refrigerator, but it lasts about a month or more. It never lasts that long in my house because it is gone in a few weeks. The original recipe calls for a can of peeled tomatoes, but they are hard to find. I use stewed tomatoes and put them in the blender so the skins get cut up and come out smooth.

Ingredients:
2 (28-oz) cans peeled tomatoes (sometimes stewed tomatoes are peeled)
1/2 cup water
2/3 cup granulated sugar
3/4 cup white vinegar
1/2 teaspoon garlic powder
1 teaspoon onion powder
1/8 teaspoon mustard powder
1/2 teaspoon salt
1/8 teaspoon celery seed
1/4 teaspoon ground pepper
1/4 teaspoon cayenne pepper
1 whole clove

Directions:
1. Prepare a Crock-Pot with a liner. The liner works better than spraying.

2. Pour the blended or peeled can of tomatoes into the bottom of the Crock-Pot and add the water.

3. Whisk in the sugar and vinegar.

4. In a bowl combine the garlic powder, onion powder, salt, celery seed, pepper and cayenne. Whisk with a dry whisk to combine. Pour into the Crock-Pot and combine all together. Drop in the whole clove.

5. Cook on high for 6 hours and stir every hour. It should be very thick when it is done.

6. Remove the clove and discard. Use an immersion blender to blend the mixture smooth. If you do not have an immersion blender, pour by measuring out by cups in a regular blender and blend.

7. Ladle the ketchup into a fine strainer and strain out any remaining seeds or skins, use the back of a ladle to press it through the strainer.

8. Cool and put in bottles or jars and refrigerate.

Meaty Spaghetti Sauce

It is no secret, I am addicted to Crock-Pots and I have several. I have them in small sizes (2-quart), I have medium size ones (5-qt) and even larger ones. When I make this spaghetti sauce, I bring out all the medium and large Crock-Pots I have and make multiple batches so we can eat one for dinner and freeze the rest of the batches for later. My whole house smells like an Italian restaurant when I do this.

Ingredients:
2 tablespoons olive oil
1 large yellow onion, peeled and chopped
2 cloves garlic, peeled and minced
1/4-pound bulk Italian sausage (use sweet, mild or hot)
1 pound lean ground beef
1 (14.5-oz) can Roma tomatoes
1 (14.5-oz) can stewed tomatoes
1 (29-oz) can of tomato sauce
1 (6-oz) can tomato paste
1 1/2 teaspoons Italian seasoning
1 tablespoon granulated sugar

Directions:
1. Put a skillet on the stove over medium heat and sauté the onion and garlic in the olive oil.

2. Add the sausage and ground beef and brown.

3. Prepare a Crock-Pot with nonstick spray.

4. Place the ingredients in the skillet in the Crock-Pot

5. Add the Roma tomatoes and stewed tomatoes along with the tomato sauce and paste.

6. Add the Italian seasoning and stir. Cook low for 8 hours.

7. About 15 minutes before serving, stir in the sugar and combine well. Serve over pasta.

Mushroom Gravy Sauce

Serve this simple sauce over egg noodles or rice or serve with roast beef and mashed potatoes. I use Baby bellas instead of button mushrooms. They are small portabella mushrooms and have a little more flavor and texture.

Ingredients:
3 tablespoons butter
2 green onions, minced (use shallots for fancy sauce)
2 cloves of garlic, peeled and minced
1 tablespoon fresh rosemary, minced
1 package button mushrooms, sliced
6 tablespoons white wine or beef broth
1 cup heavy cream
Salt and pepper to taste

Directions:
1. In a skillet, melt the butter and add the onions, garlic and rosemary. Sauté for about 3 minutes and add the mushrooms.

2. Just cook through.

3. Prepare a Crock-Pot with nonstick spray and pour the ingredients in the skillet in the Crock-Pot.

4. Pour in the wine or beef broth and heavy cream and stir.

5. Cook on low 30 minutes to 1 hour. The mixture should thicken. If it doesn't, leave the lid off and cook another 30 minutes.

No Fuss Half-Cup Cranberry Sauce

Put this on when you put your turkey in, if you slow cook it and the sauce is done before the turkey. There is a reason I call it ½ cup cranberry sauce and that is self-evident once you start to make it. It is very delicious and much better than the stuff you get in a can.

Ingredients:
1/2 cup orange juice
1/2 cup water
1/2 cup granulated sugar
1/2 cup packed brown sugar
1/2 teaspoon ground cinnamon
1/2 teaspoon grated orange peel
1 (12-oz) package fresh cranberries

Directions:
1. Use a liner in the Crock-Pot.

2. Put the orange juice and water in the bottom of the Crock-Pot and add the granulated and brown sugar. Whisk with a wire whisk.

3. Add the cinnamon and orange peel and whisk.

4. Pour in the cranberries and cook on high 3 hours, stirring every hour. This is important so the mixture will not get too cooked and brown.

5. Remove the lid and cook on high until all the cranberries pop and the sauce starts to thicken. (about 30 minutes to 1 hour)

6. Cool before serving.

Pretty in Pink Vodka Sauce

Not only is vodka sauce delicious, it is very pretty and nicely creamy. It has a mild flavor that is delightful over pasta, but especially cheese ravioli or tortellini.

Ingredients:
2 cloves garlic, peeled and minced
1 small onion, peeled and chopped fine

1 teaspoon olive oil
1 (14.5 or 15-oz) can tomato sauce
1 cup beef broth
1 cup vodka
1 (14.5-oz) can diced tomatoes (do not drain)
6 basil leaves that have been finely chopped
1/2 teaspoon crushed red pepper flakes
1/2 cup half and half
1/2 teaspoon salt
1/4 teaspoon pepper

Directions:

1. Prepare a Crock-Pot with nonstick spray.

2. Add all the ingredients except the half and half, salt and pepper and stir to combine well.

3. Cook on low 6 hours or on high for 4 hours.

4. During the last 15 minutes of cooking, whisk in the half and half, salt and pepper. Cover again and cook on high for the last 15 minutes.

5. Serve this sauce over pasta.

Slow Cooker Mexican Salsa
Salsa is cheap at the grocery store, but it doesn't always have good flavor. It is no trouble to make this salsa in a slow cooker. Keep it in the refrigerator of freeze it when done so you have it anytime.

Ingredients:
1 medium white onion, peeled and chopped
4 cloves garlic, peeled and minced
2 Jalapeño Peppers, seeded and sliced thin
¼ cup frozen and thawed corn kernels
½ a red or green bell pepper, seeded and chopped
10 Roma tomatoes
4 cloves garlic, peeled and minced
1/4 teaspoon salt
1/4 teaspoon pepper

1 tablespoon fresh lime juice
1/2 cup chopped fresh cilantro

Directions:

1. Prepare a Crock-Pot with nonstick spray

2. Place the onions in the bottom of the Crock-Pot and add the Jalapeno peppers, corn kernels and green pepper.

3. Cut a slit in 4 of the tomatoes and insert a clove of garlic in each slit. Add the tomatoes with the garlic to the Crock-Pot along with the ones that do not.

4. Add the salt and pepper and cook on high for 3 hours.

5. Spoon the tomatoes out with a slotted spoon and put in a bowl. Cover with plastic wrap and let them cool to room temperature. The skins will loosen and come off easily. Leave the rest of the ingredients in the slow cooker but turn it off and cover it. Discard the skins.

6. Pour the tomatoes into a blender with the rest of the ingredients in the Crock-Pot and pulse. You don't want it to be smooth, but you do want it to be chunky.

7. Chill for at least 2 hours and add the lime juice and cilantro. Stir and serve.

Sweet and Tangy Barbeque Sauce

This is one of the best barbeque sauce recipes I have ever made. If you have a barbeque and tell guests you are serving this sauce, they will make time to come every time. It is very sweet, yet has a tang that stays near the back of the throat and wakes up the taste buds. You need to refrigerate any leftover, if there is any leftover and it is easily frozen too. I keep several batches in the freezer and use them before 3 months is up.

Ingredients:
1 small onion, peeled and chopped fine
1 teaspoon granulated sugar
1-1/2 cup brown sugar, packed
1/2 cup prepared mustard
1 (28 oz) bottle of ketchup

1 (12=oz) bottle of beer
2 tablespoons white vinegar
1-1/2 teaspoon garlic powder
1/2 teaspoon chili powder
1/4 teaspoon curry powder
1/4 teaspoon cayenne
1 teaspoon black pepper

Directions:

1. Prepare a Crock-Pot with nonstick spray

2. Layer in all the ingredients and stir to combine well.

3. Cook on low 12 hours.

4. Let cool 1 to 2 hours and refrigerate at least 4 hours before using or freeze.

Sweetly Sinful Heavenly Apple Butter

My favorite restaurant is run by Mennonites and every table has a jar of apple butter and is served several slices of homemade bread per person. My grandmother used to make apple butter in an old cast iron pot over a fire in the backyard. She put copper pennies in the bottom to keep it from burning. It was such a pain, because you had to stir it all the time because once it burned, you had to throw it away. It tasted terrible if that happened. She employed the whole family to take a turn stirring the pot. This recipe is a far cry from the old way of making apple butter and the results are simply divine.

Ingredients:
5-1/2 pounds apples (I use Macintosh apples)
4 cups granulated sugar
1/2 teaspoon ground cloves
2-1/2 teaspoon cinnamon
1/4 teaspoon salt

Directions:

1. Prepare the Crock-Pot with nonstick spray. I actually think using a liner works a little better.

2. Peel, core and slice the apples uniformly and place them in the bottom of the Crock-Pot.

3. In a bowl, combine the sugar, cloves, cinnamon and salt and whisk together. Sprinkle over the apples and toss to coat each apple slice.

4. Cook on high for 1 hour.

5. Turn the Crock-Pot to low and cook for 10 hours. I start mine about 9 on a Saturday morning and am done around 9 at night. It is worth it. You do have to stir every hour so that it does not start to stick. You will see it thicken hour by hour.

6. Turn heat to low and cook 1 more hour without the lid on. It should really thicken now.

7. Let it cool a few hours and by 11 at night you should be able to put it in jars. Keep the apple butter refrigerated, or put it in freezer bags and stock up for when you can't get good apples.

Taco Sauce
This sauce is not like salsa. Salsa is chunky and taco sauce is smooth. It also tastes much different. Serve over enchiladas or burritos or put a little inside a Quesadilla.

Ingredients:
5 large tomatoes, peeled but do not chop
1 large yellow onions, peeled and chopped
2 cloves garlic, peeled and minced
1 jalapeno pepper, seeded and chopped
½ teaspoon Worcestershire sauce
½ tablespoon sugar
½ teaspoon chili powder
1 teaspoon salt
½ teaspoon oregano
½ teaspoon thyme
½ tablespoon flour
½ tablespoon vegetable oil
½ tablespoon white vinegar

Directions:
1. Prepare a Crock-Pot with nonstick spray or put a liner in it.

2. Put the whole peeled tomatoes in the bottom and top with onions, garlic, jalapeno, Worcestershire sauce, sugar, chili powder, salt, oregano and thyme.

3. Stir and cook on low 8 to 10 hours.

4. Turn on high during the last hour.

5. In a bowl, whisk together the flour, vegetable oil and white vinegar until smooth. Pour this into the Crock-Pot and stir to mix it in with the rest of the ingredients.

6. Scoop out into a blender or use an immersion blender to blend smooth.

7. Put in a jar to cool and keep in the refrigerator until it is used.

Tomato Horseradish Sauce

We like this sauce over meatballs or on our hamburgers and hotdogs. It has some punch to it and is different than plain old ketchup. The instant tapioca is what thickens this sauce and makes it creamy.

Ingredients:
1 (10.75-oz) can condensed tomato soup
1 (4-oz) can tomato juice
2 cups water
3 tablespoons Worcestershire sauce
2 tablespoons prepared horseradish
1 tablespoon Dijon mustard
2 tablespoons dried parsley
¼ cup dry onion flakes
2 teaspoons garlic powder
¼ teaspoon pepper
3 tablespoons instant tapioca

Directions:
1. Put a liner in the Crock-Pot.

2. Combine all ingredients in the Crock-Pot and whisk well to combine.

3. Cook on low 3 to 4 hours or until it thickens.

Conclusion

Get those Crock-Pots and slow cookers out of the kitchen cupboards and off the top of your refrigerator and start using them! You will save money, time and energy by using a Crock-Pot rather than a regular oven or stove top. Get everything ready the night before, put the ingredients in the pot in the morning, turn it on and have a delicious meal when you get home from work. No more trips to the fast food restaurants or ordering pizza because you have a delicious and nutritious meal waiting for you as you walk in the door. Just prepare a few side dishes or additions that only take a few minutes and dinner is on the table. One of the best things is that you only have one crock to wash instead of a bunch of pots and pans afterwards. I hope you enjoy these recipes for many years to come.

Thanks for reading. If this book helped you or someone you know in any way, then please spare a few moments right now to leave a nice review.

My Other Books

Be sure to check out my author page to learn more about me and see my other books at:

USA:
https://www.amazon.com/author/susanhollister

UK: http://amzn.to/2qiEzA9

Or simply type my name in the search bar: Susan Hollister

Thank You

CPSIA information can be obtained
at www.ICGtesting.com
Printed in the USA
LVOW09s0044171217

560051LV00020B/640/P